JEWELLERY

Miranda Innes

JEWELLERY

Photography by Clive Streeter

DORLING KINDERSLEY
LONDON · NEW YORK · STUTTGART · MOSCOW

A DORLING KINDERSLEY BOOK

Created and produced by
COLLINS & BROWN LIMITED
London House
Great Eastern Wharf
Parkgate Road
London SW11 4NQ

Project Editor	Heather Dewhurst
Managing Editor	Sarah Hoggett
Editorial Assistant	Corinne Asghar
Art Director	Roger Bristow
Art Editor	Marnie Searchwell
Photography	Clive Streeter
Stylist	Ali Edney

First published in Great Britain in 1996
by Dorling Kindersley Limited
9 Henrietta Street, London WC2E 8PS

A CIP catalogue record for this book is available
from the British Library.

ISBN 0 7513 0297 X

Reproduced by Daylight Colour Art in Singapore
Printed and bound in France by Pollina - n° 68961 - A

Contents

Introduction 6
Basic Materials 8
Fastenings and Tools 10

Paper and Fabric Jewellery

Introduction 12
Paper Rainbows 14
Pebble Necklace 18
Star-spangled Stunner 22
Patchwork Bangle 26
Felt Baubles 30
Magic Earrings 34
Kaleidoscope Necklet 38
Renaissance Riches 42
Ideas to Inspire 46

Beads and Glass Jewellery

Introduction 50
Millefiori
Mosaic Beads 52
Stained Glass
Pendant 56
Four-stranded
Necklace 60
Glittering Regalia 64
Ideas to Inspire 68

Wood and Metal Jewellery

Introduction 72
Copper Leaf
Brooch 74
Painted Tin Brooch 78
Mixed Media
Brooch 82
Etched Metal
Earrings 86
Ideas to Inspire 90

Contributors 94
Index 95
Suppliers 96
Acknowledgments 96

Introduction

JEWELLERY FALLS roughly into two categories – the sort that requires an armed guard, and the sort that has no other purpose than to give you a frisson of pleasure. This is not the book for people who feel naked without a sheik's ransom of diamonds about their person, rather it is for anyone who wants to look like a million dollars for the price of a daily paper. Within its pages, you will find the key to making perfectly respectable necklaces and earrings, beads, bangles, and brooches, along with a few forays into the wilder interpretations of jewellery, and one or two bold examples of delightful kitsch. The whole spectrum of brilliant and glittering bijoux, baubles, and gewgaws is covered, apart from the most serious. All jewellery should be fun, as well as being decorative, and actually making it yourself doubles the satisfaction.

None of the projects in this book costs as much as a minuscule

Rainbow Colours
Brightly painted stripes, spots, and squiggles adorn a wooden brooch.

pair of gold ear-studs, most do not need expensive equipment, and a few hours is plenty of time to make any of them. Some of the designs are more classic than others – you may find that your children will covet some of the pieces – and one or two of them are unashamedly contemporary fashion items; however, the techniques can easily be adapted to suit whatever is the current essential accessory.

Many of the techniques shown in the book may hark back to your childhood. Rolled paper beads are an example; while no one could call them sophisticated, they are fun to make and great to wear on holiday. Papier mâché is another fine kindergarten pastime that resurfaces in a more glamorous guise in jewellery-making, and may evoke misty reminiscences as you pulp your paper and transform it with paint and gilding. Vanishing muslin is a more recent and technological discovery; lacy, cobweb-fine pieces can be made simply using colourful

Painted Tin
These welded tin brooches are painted with glossy enamel paints.

Harlequin Scraps
Bright snippets and scraps of fabric create a brilliant patchwork bangle in jester's motley.

embroidery thread and a sewing machine, following a technique that results in a glossy cross between satin and lace, embellished with tiny beads or sequins as you wish. Felt is another fabric with potential; it is the oldest man-made textile and was all the rage in the better class of cave, but there is nothing primitive about the brilliant baubles we show you how to make.

A close perusal of the gallery sections will fill you with further ideas, building on those you may already have dreamed up. Beading using thin wire instead of thread, for example, confers a rigid structure that might be exactly what you need to make an unassuming yet stylish crown for occasions when a touch of the regal is required. In fact, once you get the hang of this technique, you could find yourself turning out chokers and chandeliers. Mosaic techniques also adapt to all kinds of objects, and can be built up using resin, or on a more durable base of metal or wood if you have a mind to make a glittering picture frame.

This book gives you the basic recipes, upon which you can invent variations to

Newsy Necklace
The printed word provides the decoration in this inventive papier mâché necklace.

Bright Baubles
Pre-dyed woollen fleece and shiny studs combine in an original pair of earrings.

your heart's content. You will soon begin to see shining possibilities in the most unexpected places. The seashore will become a treasure trove, with new glories thrown up by every passing tide. Mundane trips to the ironmongers and hardware stores will induce an overwhelming state of trance as you size up the possibilities of that copper wire, or those wing-nuts. Haberdashery departments will have you mesmerized with their rainbow stacks of silks, glossy threads, sequins, beads, and buttons. You might even find yourself exploring the musty hinterland of charity shops in search of abandoned necklaces and broken bracelets to recycle into dazzling and original brooches and hat pins. As you begin to extend your tool kit and add such invaluable items as tin snips, superglue, round-nosed pliers, and earring findings, you will start to notice the clever little touches that complete a piece of jewellery and give it a professional air. This book will start you off making your own jewellery, and give you ideas enough to keep you coruscating throughout many a party season.

Light Show
Coloured glass and bright droplets add a glowing luminosity to jewellery.

Basic Materials

YOU CAN MAKE stunning jewellery with very little outlay using the most basic of materials. Simply with coloured paper and paint, you can make papier mâché or rolled paper bead necklaces, interspersing with wooden or glass beads. Alternatively, you can collect remnants of fabric, and stitch soft padded earrings and brooches, and embellish these with beads and embroidery. If you have a toolbox handy, you could tackle thin wood, sheet copper, steel, or brass to create and decorate jewellery. Coloured sheet glass is another wonderful material you can use, either shaped with a glass cutter for

Fancy beads

◄ **Glass and Beads**
Coloured or mirror glass is excellent for mosaic pieces and is easily cut to the desired shape with a glass cutter. Beads come in every colour and material. Simply thread them on to waxed polyester or wire to make foolproof jewellery.

Coloured and mirror glass

Wooden beads

Pressed leaves

▼ **Paper and Cardboard**
Use coloured and plain paper, even newspaper, to make and decorate your jewellery. Cardboard makes an ideal base for papier mâché brooches and earrings.

Glass nuggets

Raffia

Seed beads

Waxed thread

◄ **Threading Materials**
Use waxed thread or nylon-coated miniature wire cable to thread strands of lightweight or tiny seed beads to make necklaces and bangles. Raffia is an ideal material for larger, heavier beads, and has a more textured and natural, earthy appearance.

Assorted papers and cardboard

Miniature wire cable

mosaic jewellery or wrapped with channelled lead for stained glass pieces. Decorate your jewellery with paints, inks, silks, threads, pressed leaves, haberdashery or ironmongery. The one essential material you need for threading beads is waxed thread or miniature wire cable; alternatively, you could use raffia.

▼ Fabrics
Hessian is the base for hand-hooked jewellery; vanishing muslin is used in machine embroidery. You can make all manner of sumptuous baubles from pieces of silk and fabric scraps, or bright, chunky felt beads from pre-dyed woollen fleece.

Hessian

◄ Paints and Inks
Paper jewellery can be quickly transformed with a coat of paint. Gouache is best for paper; acrylics work well on wood and metal. Coloured inks are a good alternative on wood, allowing the grain to show through.

Acrylic and gouache paints

Water-based ink

Vanishing muslin

Silks

► Threads
You have the whole spectrum at your disposal when you use threads to embellish your jewellery, and a range of textures from glistening metallic threads through to silky, stranded embroidery skeins.

Metallic thread

Stranded embroidery thread

▼ Metals and Wood
Sheet metal and thin wood are easy to work with, provided you have the right tools. Channelled lead is perfect for wrapping around pieces of glass, while metal tubing can be used to make decorative rivets.

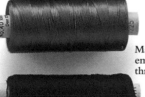

Machine embroidery threads

Fabric scraps

eet copper, el, and ass

Thin balsa wood

Silver tubing

Channelled lead

Sanded sheet steel

Pre-dyed fleece

Fastenings and Tools

ONCE YOU HAVE MADE the decorative part of your jewellery, you will need to attach a fastening to it, to enable you to wear it. There is a wide variety of findings, pins, rings, hooks, and wires readily available for you to choose from. Depending on the type of jewellery you are making, you will also need various tools to shape, cut, and polish your pieces. With a bit of ingenuity you can make do with what you have at home to begin with, then gradually collect more items as and when you need them.

▶ Fastenings

There are all sorts of fastenings available, in a huge variety of shapes and styles. You can use them alone, to complete your jewellery, or in conjunction with each other, to link elements together. Use findings or bolt and split rings for necklaces, hooks for earrings, and pins for brooches. Bell caps are useful for tidying up ragged ends.

Earring findings

Split rings

Brooch pins

Necklace findings

Bell cap fastenings

Bolt rings

Hat pins

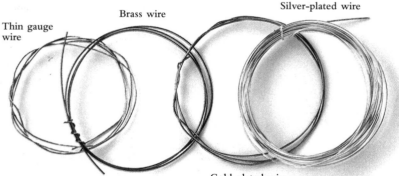

Thin gauge wire

Brass wire

Silver-plated wire

Gold-plated wire

◀ Wires

Wire is essential in jewellery making and can have several purposes. You can loop wire with pliers to hook elements of a necklace or bracelet together, or thread beads on to wire to add another section to earrings. You can also make decorative coils to add to earrings, necklaces, or hat pins.

Hook

◀ Sewing Tools

Pins and needles are vital for making fabric jewellery. A fine beading needle is perfect for sewing tiny beads on to fabric. For embroidery, stretch the fabric in a hoop. A hook is needed to pull loops of fabric through coarse hessian.

Beading needles

Pins

Drill

Fine sewing scissors

Dressmaking scissors

Fid

Embroidery hoop

► Skewers and Sticks

Cocktail sticks are very useful for positioning tiny pieces of decoration; wooden skewers can hold beads while they are drying; and knitting needles are good for wrapping paper around to make rolled beads.

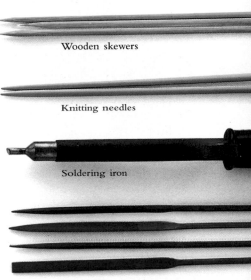

Cocktail sticks

Wooden skewers

Knitting needles

Soldering iron

Metal files

▼ Solder and Flux

There are different types of solder and flux but they all fuse metal to metal. Apply the flux to the surface of the metal, then, holding both pieces of metal together, melt the solder on top to fuse them.

Solder

Flux

► Punching Tools

You can create wonderful textured patterns on metal using a hammer and centre punch. Place the metal on an anvil, hold a centre punch vertically on the metal, and hammer it sharply. Repeat to create a surface pitted with dots.

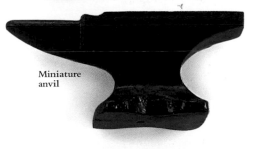

Hammer and centre punch

▼ Cutting and Shaping Tools

Dressmaking scissors are essential for cutting large areas of fabric; smaller scissors are useful for fine work. A scalpel is good for cutting paper and cardboard. You need a glass cutter for cutting glass for mosaic jewellery. To cut wood or metal, use a piercing saw — you may need a drill to make holes before sawing. Tin snips can also be used to cut metal. Use metal files to smooth the cut edges. Pliers are useful for bending and shaping wire into loops and hooks. A fid is used to press chanelled lead securely on to the edge of a piece of glass.

Pumice powder

Miniature anvil

► Polishing Tools

Use pumice powder on a brass brush moistened with water to burnish sheet metals. Give your jewellery a final shine with a glass brush before polishing with a soft cloth.

Brass brush and glass brush

Metal ruler

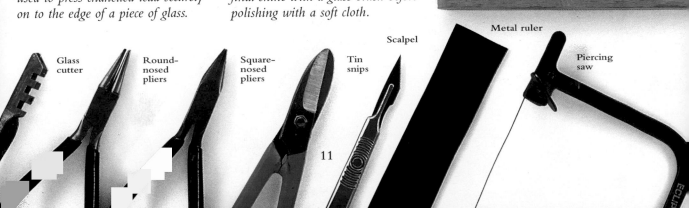

Glass cutter

Round-nosed pliers

Square-nosed pliers

Tin snips

Scalpel

Piercing saw

Paper and Fabric Jewellery

·····································

THE JEWELLERY IN THIS SECTION is likely to cost you almost nothing, and to require very little equipment, making it perfect for beginners. Paper beads are one example; nothing could be much simpler or more magical than transforming magazines into confetti-bright carnival necklaces. Papier mâché jewellery can be covered with bright paint, sweet wrappers, fake gems, and gilding, with results that can look like mysterious archeaological relics or designer bijoux, depending on how refined you care to be. Scrap bangles and brooches made by rag-rug methods are not a lot more complicated, and they share the satisfying advantage of being recycled, while extremely glamorous earrings and collars can be made using nothing more demanding than coloured thread and a sewing machine. Once you start, you will be thrilled by how much can be made from so little.

Paper Rainbows

MATERIALS

Sheets of
coloured paper
PVA glue
Wooden beads
Waxed thread

EQUIPMENT

Ruler
Pen
Scissors
Artist's brush
Fine knitting needle
Wooden skewers
Dish

AS ADORNMENT GOES, there are few things simpler than rolled paper beads. Any child can make them, and any adult with a sense of drama could wear them with panache. Beloved of our great-grandmothers, paper beads utilize the most basic commodities that most people can stretch to – bright paper and glue. From these lowly beginnings, splendid results follow.

Magazines can yield polychrome pages for free, but if you take a look in any shop selling wrapping paper you will see an Aladdin's cave of brilliant possibilities. There are handmade papers in subtle hues and refined textures, bright, smooth kraft papers, papers inlaid with glittering confetti in gold and silver, and paper patterned with colourful marbled, mottled, metallic, and speckled designs.

If your jewels cost nothing, you can afford to be generous; rolled paper beads look good in quantity. Vary the shape of your beads by cutting differently shaped paper triangles, and dip them in tinted varnish instead of colourless PVA. You can't go far wrong with paper; you can make anything from huge rough beads to tiny shiny ones. There is every excuse to experiment and enjoy yourself.

Festival Necklace
As joyful and theatrical as mardi gras, *this kaleidoscopic collar is carnival and Christmas rolled into one.*

Party Colours
By choosing different spacers and coloured papers, combining many strands or just one, and varying the size of the beads, you can create dozens of easy variations on this jaunty theme.

Making the Beads
You do not need great artistic skill to make paper beads;
even children can make them. All you need are magazines,
scissors, a dab of glue, and a knitting needle.

Colourful
magazine pages

Waxed thread

PVA glue

Wooden beads
and spacers

1 *Search through magazines for colourful pages and cut them out. Sort the pages into toning colours. Take one sheet at a time and divide it into triangles. To do this, mark every 5cm (2in) along one edge. Repeat on the opposite edge of the paper, but this time starting 2.5cm (1in) in from the side. Using a ruler and pen, join up the marks on opposite edges of the paper to make long, narrow triangles.*

2 *Cut out the triangles with a pair of sharp scissors. Each triangle will make one bead. To make a necklace about 75cm (30in) long, you will need approximately 24 beads.*

3 *Check which side of the paper is the most colourful. Turn the triangles over and paint PVA glue on the reverse side, starting about 3cm (1¼in) from the base and gluing to the tip. Glue three triangles at a time, before proceeding on to the next step.*

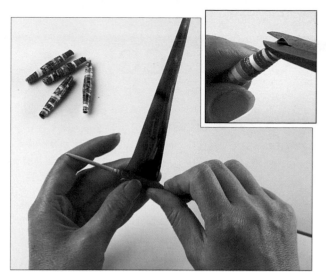

4 *Wrap the unglued end of a paper triangle around a knitting needle. Roll up the paper tightly around the needle. When you reach the tip, pull the knitting needle out and clip off any untidy ends with scissors (see inset). Repeat with each triangle and leave the rolled beads to dry.*

5 *When the beads are dry, insert three at a time on a wooden skewer, spacing them apart. Using an artist's brush, paint each bead all over with a coat of PVA glue, which acts as a varnish. Prop the skewers over a dish and leave the beads to dry for an hour.*

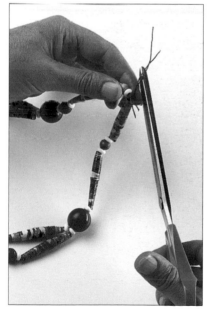

6 *Choose wooden beads to tone with the paper beads. Thread one strand of beads on waxed thread, alternating paper beads with wooden beads. Repeat to thread a second, shorter strand. These strands will be joined together to make one necklace, so choose beads that complement each other. Leave 20cm (8in) of thread free at each end for knotting.*

7 *Join the two strands of beads together at each end by threading both strands through one wooden bead on each end. Then thread a further three or four beads on to the doubled strands at each end of the necklace.*

8 *Knot the four threads together securely. Trim the ends of the thread with scissors, then paint the knot with PVA glue for extra security. Push the knot inside a paper bead so that it is not visible and move all the beads around the thread accordingly.*

Pebble Necklace

MATERIALS

Nylon cord
Matt adhesive tape
Nylon thread
Raffia
Assorted pebble beads
Natural linen thread
2 bell cap fastenings
Split ring
PVA glue
Bolt ring

EQUIPMENT

Scissors
Tape measure
Needle
Large-eyed needle
Cocktail stick

THIS BEACHCOMBER'S COLLECTION of pebbles and raffia is put together with casual grace, making it the perfect necklace for summer. If you are adept with power tools, you could make a wearable souvenir of lazy summer days using real pebbles or shells collected on the shoreline instead of beads. Drill a hole in the pebbles using a fine masonry bit, then thread them together with fine linen yarn or gardening twine.

Making this necklace involves the technique of wrapping; here raffia and linen thread are used to give an earthy, natural look, but you could also try using coloured linen, or embroidery silk allied with glass droplets and metal beads, to produce something rich and festive. Once you feel confident with wrapping, you can use it for lustrous plaited cords with which you can make chokers, or even belts if ambition grips you. What distinguishes this necklace from the one that a child might have made is the attention to details; the linen spiral is applied very evenly over the raffia, and the neat closure with metal bell caps makes a huge difference to the finished necklace.

Seaside Chic
Easy to make and easy to wear, this necklace will be your favourite summer accessory. When the nights draw in, you will be cheeringly reminded of hot sun and the sound of the waves every time you catch sight of it.

Desert Detritus
Terracotta and bone are perfectly juxtaposed in this talismanic necklace. Such classy flotsam could be interspersed equally effectively with frosted and stone-washed glass or buttons.

Assembling the Necklace
*The elements of this necklace — the pebble beads, raffia,
and linen thread — make you think of summer.*

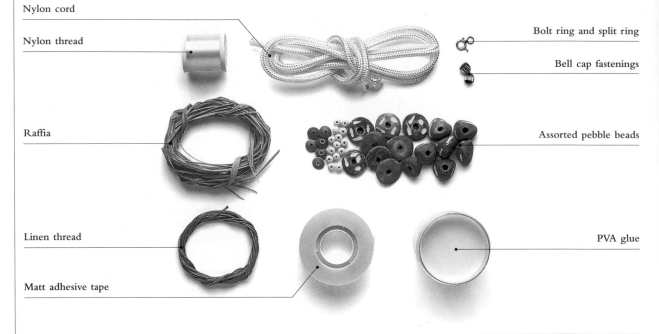

Nylon cord

Nylon thread

Bolt ring and split ring

Bell cap fastenings

Raffia

Assorted pebble beads

Linen thread

PVA glue

Matt adhesive tape

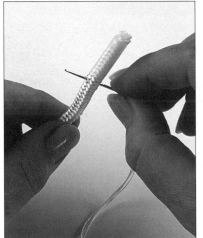

1 Cut a 45cm (18in) piece of nylon cord. Wrap matt adhesive tape around each end. Thread a needle with doubled nylon thread, 25cm (10in) long. Pass the needle through the cord, 2.5cm (1in) from one end; pull it until the thread is centred. Cut the thread; remove the needle. Tape the centre of the thread to the cord; knot the thread ends together. Repeat at the other end of the cord. These threads should remain free.

2 Taking a length of raffia, lay the end of it along one end of the cord. Begin to wrap the raffia around the cord, covering and securing the end of the raffia as you go. Wrap evenly, leaving no visible gaps. As you reach the end of a length of raffia, place the end against the first 5cm (2in) of the new length, and wrap over the top to conceal the ends. Continue wrapping in this way until the entire length of the cord is covered.

3 To secure the raffia at the end of the cord, thread a large-eyed needle with the raffia and push the needle back between the cord and its wrapping for about 2.5cm (1in). Bring the needle out, and cut the raffia close to the wrapping.

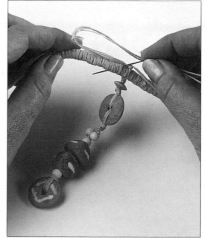

4 *Make a beaded section to hang from the wrapped cord. Fold a length of raffia in half. Thread the looped end through a flat-disc pebble bead, pass the two raffia ends through the loop and tighten. Thread several pebble beads on to the doubled raffia, then split the raffia and thread a bead on to each strand. Knot each strand.*

5 *Knot the two strands together. Pass the raffia strands singly through the centre of a flat-disc bead, one from the front and one from the back of the bead, so that the strands cross in the hole. Knot the strands together directly above the disc, then thread on another bead and knot the raffia to complete the section.*

6 *Tie the beaded section securely on to the centre of the wrapped cord. Using a large-eyed needle, thread the raffia ends through the wrapping on each side of the knot and cut close to the wrapped cord. Attach more beaded sections to the cord on each side of the central hanging beaded section, as above.*

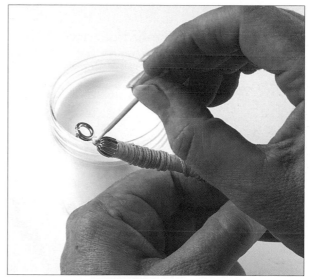

7 *Starting about 2cm (¾in) in from one end of the cord, lay linen thread against the raffia-covered cord and wrap it around the cord as before. After approximately 2cm (¾in) of wrapping, make a long diagonal wrap so as to leave about 1.5cm (⅝in) of raffia showing, before wrapping another section of 2cm (¾in). Continue like this until you reach the hanging beaded section and wrap more densely here, leaving the knots as a feature. Wrap until you reach the end of the cord, then finish off as in step 3.*

8 *Thread the four strands of nylon thread at one end of the necklace through a bell cap fastening; slide the bell cap down to cover the end of the cord. Thread a split ring on to two of the strands of nylon and knot all four strands to secure. Cut the ends and, using a cocktail stick, dab with PVA glue to seal. Thread a bell cap on to the other end of the cord, as before. Thread two of the four strands of nylon through the end loop of a bolt ring, knot securely, cut the ends, and seal with PVA glue. Leave to dry.*

Star-spangled Stunner

MATERIALS
Cardboard
Hessian
Fabric strips, 12mm
(½in) wide
Foil strips, 12mm
(½in) wide
Latex adhesive
Clear adhesive
Black felt
Black sewing thread
Brooch pin
Superglue

EQUIPMENT
Scissors
Marker pen
Embroidery frame
Hook
Needle

EVERYONE KNOWS that recycling is worthy, but some people have found the secret of making it fun. An inauspicious trio of thrift-shop fabric, hessian, and old crisp packets has been transformed into this star brooch of stylish, insouciant braggadocio, which has the great added advantage of being shamelessly showy, yet unlikely to attract muggers or to need stowing nightly in the safe.

If you have never experienced the immense smug pleasure of making something from nothing, this is your chance. This brooch is a miniature version of the rag rugs with which our grandparents used to cheat penury and icy winter draughts. You could use any materials; bright felt, wool, old T-shirts, shiny satin, or Thai silk would all have a particular and attractive quality. Here the dark fabric is in witty counterpoint to the plastic foil, which produces a texture and steely glint reminiscent of chain mail. In the bad old days, it took an entire winter to make a hearthrug. This handsome star could grace your lapel in a matter of hours; if you prefer, you could make a hooked heart or daisy, or even a Christmas tree.

Star Attraction
This star brooch does not belong to the discreetly priceless category of jewellery; it is designed to be worn with a smile and to be greeted with a giggle.

Loop Story
If old crisp packets and strips of fabric can be said to dance, these brooches have a definite funky rhythm. For extra sparkle, you could sew on a sprinkling of sequins.

Hooking the Star

*Achieving even loops will become easy with a little
practice, and you can raid your scrap-bag for appealing
colours and textures of fabric.*

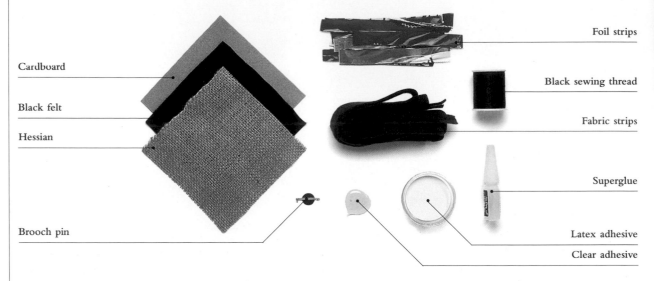

Cardboard

Black felt

Hessian

Brooch pin

Foil strips

Black sewing thread

Fabric strips

Superglue

Latex adhesive

Clear adhesive

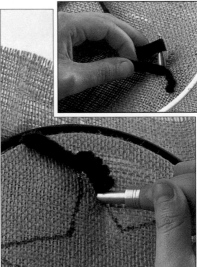

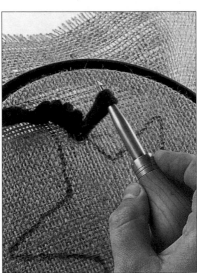

1 *Make a cardboard template of the
shape of your brooch. This brooch
design is a star, but you could choose
any shape you like. Using a marker
pen, draw around this shape on to a
piece of hessian, leaving a border of at
least 7.5cm (3in) around your design.*

2 *Put the hessian in an embroidery
frame so that the design lies
centrally in the frame. Begin hooking
fabric strips around the outline of the
star. Hold the fabric strip beneath the
hessian with one hand, then push the
hook through the hessian from above
with the other hand. Guide the fabric
strip over the hook to create a loop
(see inset). Pull the hook back through
the hessian, bringing the end of the
fabric strip to the top side.*

3 *Push the hook back through the
hessian just next to the strip,
guide the fabric on to the hook and
pull it through the hessian to the top
side, creating a loop on the surface of
the hessian. Pull the fabric strip back
gently until the loop is at the required
height. Continue forming a line of
loops in this way around the star. At
the end of a fabric strip, bring the end
through to the top side of the hessian
and trim to the height of the loops.*

4 *Once you have completed an outline around the star shape, begin to hook foil strips in the centre of the star, working from the centre outwards until you have filled the design. Ensure that the foil loops are an even height.*

5 *Remove the hessian from the frame and lay it face-down on a flat surface. Cut the excess hessian away to leave a border of 2.5cm (1in) around the star shape. Using a piece of cardboard, smear a thin layer of latex adhesive over the back of the star shape and on to the border.*

6 *Using scissors, make diagonal cuts into the hessian border of the star shape, right up to the hooked area. Fold the hessian in towards the centre of the star shape, squeezing it together so that it sticks down. Trim off any excess hessian. Leave the star shape to dry for 10 minutes until the glue becomes clear.*

7 *Apply a thin layer of clear adhesive on the back of the star. Stick a piece of black felt over the glue. Trim away the excess felt around the edge of the star shape. Using a needle and black thread, slip stitch the felt to the edge of the star to secure the felt further and neaten the brooch. Attach a brooch pin to the centre back of the brooch using superglue (see inset). Leave the glue to dry for an hour before wearing the brooch.*

Patchwork Bangle

MATERIALS

Scraps of brightly
coloured fabric

Strip of calico,
30 x 5cm (12 x 2in)

Coloured
cotton thread

2 strips of plain fabric,
30 x 2.5cm
(12 x 1in)

String

Wadding

Sewing thread

Contrasting fabric
cut on the bias, 30 x
7.5cm (12 x 3in)

Stranded
embroidery thread

EQUIPMENT

Scissors

Pins

Sewing machine
and darning foot

Needle

RAID YOUR SCRAP-BAG for tiny snippets and scraps of fabric and stitch a rainbow with brightly coloured cotton. Unlike most other bangles, which advertise your approach with their racket and nearly cut off your circulation if you try to write, this one is light, flexible, soft, and silent – but by no means quiet. An armful of these bangles, as bright as a jar of jelly beans, would be unlikely to go unnoticed, and for very little outlay you could sport an impressive array of bracelets.

There are endless variations to explore. Try using fabric in shades of a single colour, for example you could take indigo and white and use every kind of spot, check, stripe, or pattern that you can lay hands on in those colours. Decorate your bangle with fancy ribbons or beads, or explore the potential of your sewing machine, and try some of those embroidery stitches that you have never found a use for. Because the raw materials cost almost nothing and the labour involved is minimal, making this bangle is a chance to be adventurous. If you are determined to be practical, you can always use washable fabrics and feel secure in the knowledge that you can put your bangle through the washing machine should it ever get dirty.

Scrap Circle

As bright and sassy as patchwork can be, this bangle flaunts the casual expertise with vivid colour and playful piecing that comes after much experience with fabrics. Leave punctilious neatness for petit-point purses, and enjoy this piece for its exuberance.

Well Wrought Wrists

Made from a cheerful, magpie motley of different colours and kinds of fabric, punctuated by bright stitching, these bangles look good in great clashing armfuls.

Sewing the Bangle

Spread out all your tattered remnants and pick a sizzling kaleidoscope of the brightest and best. Make sure that your bangle is big enough to squeeze into.

Brightly coloured fabric

String

Wadding

Calico

Sewing thread

Coloured cotton thread

Stranded embroidery thread

Contrasting fabric cut on the bias

Plain fabric

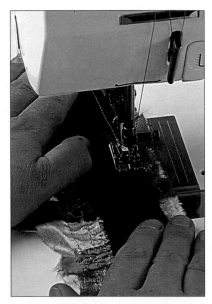

1 *Cut out or tear small rectangles of brightly coloured fabric, measuring approximately 7.5 X 2.5cm (3 X 1in). Fraying the edges will add texture to the bangle. Pin the coloured fabric scraps on to a strip of calico approximately 30cm (12in) long. Layer them on top of each other to build up a richly decorated surface.*

2 *Thread a sewing machine with coloured cotton thread. With the machine on free embroidery or darning setting, stitch across the fabric patches in different directions to secure them to the strip of calico.*

3 *With right sides together, pin and stitch the outer edge of a strip of plain fabric down one side of the patched strip. Stitch a second plain strip to the other side of the patched strip. Fold back the two plain strips to reveal a 2.5cm (1in) wide area of pattern in the centre of the patched strip, bordered with plain fabric. Trim the edges of the coloured fabric.*

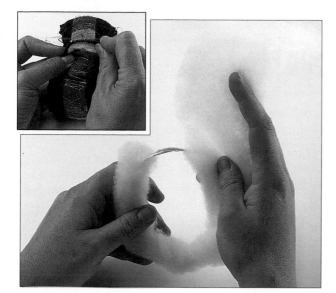

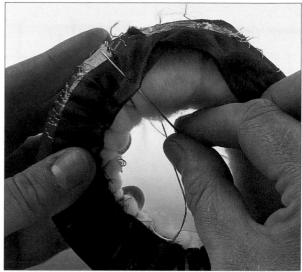

4 *Make a double loop of string large enough for your hand to pass through with a bit extra. Knot the loop. Wrap wadding firmly around the loop. Stitch the end in place to prevent the wadding unravelling. Wrap the patched strip around the outer edge of the padded loop, and slip stitch the two ends together with sewing thread (see inset).*

5 *Using sewing thread, stitch the two inner edges of the patched strip to the bangle, stitching through the wadding and pulling the thread tightly. The fabric will begin to pucker, but continue to stitch as regularly as possible. Cut out a strip of contrasting fabric approximately 25cm (10in) long and 5cm (2in) wide.*

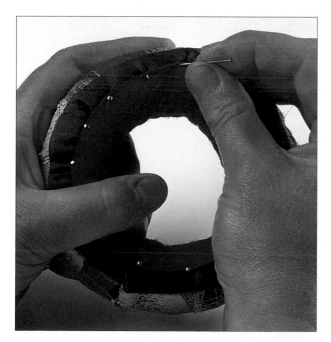

6 *Turn under the edge of the contrasting fabric and pin it around the inner edge of the bangle to conceal the stitches made in step 5 and part of the plain fabric edges. Stretching the fabric as you go, pin it at close intervals, sticking the pins down into the wadding. Repeat on the other side of the bangle, so that the fabric fits smoothly around the inside. Slip stitch the contrasting fabric in place.*

7 *Thread a needle with a contrasting colour of stranded embroidery thread. Sew the edges of the two plain-coloured fabrics together with a tiny running stitch, pinching the edges together as you go.*

Felt Baubles

MATERIALS

Pre-dyed fleece
Washing powder
Water
Nylon-coated
miniature wire cable
Necklace finding
Crimp beads

EQUIPMENT

Bowl
Scalpel
Needle
Long-nosed pliers
Wire cutters

WOOL IS A VERY UNLIKELY component of jewellery, but these giant felt beads have an unexpected extrovert appeal. The colour is so rich, the texture so dense, the completed item so light to wear, and so dramatic to look at, that you may have to reconsider all your preconceptions as to what constitutes jewellery.

There is a mysterious aspect to the making of these marbled, woollen ping-pong balls; you will discover the strange desire of wool strands to turn themselves into perfect spheres. You will also end up with very clean hands indeed. The wool you use is available pre-dyed in a range of rich colours. To make a necklace, simply alternate one or two different-coloured beads, or create a whole rainbow. For variety, use different sizes of woollen balls in partnership with each other, or embellish them with regularly spaced or patterned sequins and tiny pins, studs, or beads. You could cut them in half and either use them with their swirling middles exposed, or pair them up with a different-coloured hemisphere to make a bicoloured ball.

Sharp Spheres
Viridian, magenta, and black make a startling trio that marries perfectly with a look of snappy sophistication. Just take a sleek black suit with an unmistakable designer look, a hefty flash of panache, and these brilliant baubles, and you will make an impression wherever you go.

Black and White and Round All Over
Black and white always look good together, and these swirling felt beads are no exception — they would look perfect worn with plain, bright colours, or subtle autumn shades.

30

Making the Collar

This necklace is a winter adornment – it is comfortingly warm to wear, and decidedly warm to make.

Necklace finding

Crimp beads

Nylon-coated miniature wire cable

Washing powder

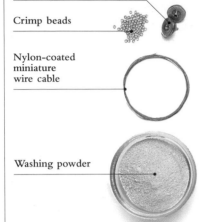

Pre-dyed fleece

1 *Pull a piece of fleece about 15cm (6in) long off a hank of pre-dyed green fleece. Wrap it together with a similar-sized piece of pink fleece, twisting the two colours together in your hands to combine them. Wrap them around and around to make a tight ball. Put on one side. Repeat to make about 15 balls.*

2 *Pull several thin strands of black fleece off a hank and wrap them individually around some of the pink and green balls for added decoration. Repeat the process with thin strands of pink and green fleece, if desired. Do not worry about securing the ends; these will be secured when the fleece is made into felt.*

3 *Mix washing powder with hot water in a bowl until the water is very frothy. Dip a fleece ball into the soapy water, then rub it between your hands to turn it into felt. Rub it gently at first, then gradually increase the pressure, dipping the ball into the soapy water periodically to keep it damp. When the ball is hard and compact, and you are no longer able to squeeze it, it is ready. This takes at least 15 minutes per ball. Repeat with each fleece ball.*

4 *Rinse the felt balls in clear water, squeezing out the bubbles. Keep changing the water in the bowl, or rinse the balls under running water. Continue to rinse until all the soap bubbles have been washed out.*

5 *Using a scalpel, cut a few of the felt balls in half. The open halves will reveal the patterns made by the different colours of fleece.*

6 *Unroll a length of nylon-coated miniature wire cable and, without cutting it off the roll, thread it through the eye of a needle. Thread the needle through one half of a necklace finding. Next take the needle through two crimp beads to thread them on to the wire, butting the beads up against the necklace finding. Then push the needle through each felt bead and half-bead in turn to wire the beads together to make the necklace.*

7 *Thread on two crimp beads, then the other half of the necklace finding. Bend the wire back and trim the wire with wire cutters at each end of the necklace. At each end, push the crimp beads down towards the finding, over the cut end of the wire, so they butt up against the finding (see inset). Using pliers, flatten the crimp beads to secure. Then snip off the end of the wire with wire cutters to neaten the necklace.*

Magic Earrings

MATERIALS

Vanishing muslin

Machine
embroidery threads

Metallic thread

Strong cotton thread
in outline colour

Variety of small beads

Gold-plated
jewellery wire

2 gold ear wires

EQUIPMENT

Felt-tip pen

Sewing machine
and darning foot

Old towel

Iron

Sharp sewing scissors

Fine or
beading needle

Wire cutters

Round-nosed pliers

THE MAGIC IN THIS CASE is a product of technology. The rich, shimmering fabric of these earrings speckled with gold and silver beads is simply a fine lacy web of machine stitching from which the dull backing fabric has been burned away. (An alternative disappearing backing fabric, featured on pp.44–45, dissolves in water.) This technique introduces a new arena of design because you are actually creating your fabric from threads – and seeing the muslin vanish is as close to magic as jewellery can get. As you become proficient with the technique, you can tackle larger and more intricate pieces; the designer who created these earrings also makes elaborate collars, brooches, and hat pins.

To see the breathtaking polychrome potential of stitching your own fabric, you only have to admire the glossy spectrum of coloured embroidery threads that beckons in any haberdasher's. You can pick from any combination of colours under the sun, and experiment with different kinds of thread, from silk and cotton to metallic. The finished earrings are light and glamorous and a pleasure to wear.

Beaded Pageantry
These earrings have an air of medieval finery. Their charm comes from a simple design intricately finished, and from the strong harmonious colours of the stitching. Good Queen Bess would have had a cabinet full of these if only they had been invented.

Intricate Stitches
Made with the same basic ingredients – vanishing muslin with a fine overlay of machine stitches and tiny, brightly-coloured beads – these embroidered earrings have subtly different effects depending on their shape and colour.

Embroidering the Earrings

You would be wise to practise stitching before you commit yourself to hours of patient machining. The beads are easy to attach, and give a delicate finish.

Metallic thread

Vanishing muslin

Strong cotton thread in outline colour

Gold-plated jewellery wire

Gold ear wires

Variety of small beads

Machine embroidery threads

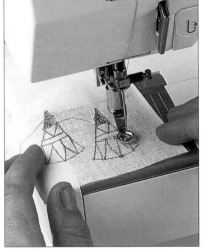

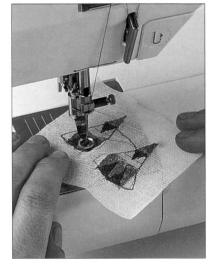

1 *Using a felt-tip pen, draw your earring design on to a piece of vanishing muslin. It is best to stick to simple shapes such as triangles or squares to begin with, as it is easier to stitch these. As you become more confident, you can tackle more intricate shapes. Decide which colours you will be using in the design; a limited palette of three or four colours at most produces the best results.*

2 *Thread the sewing machine with the first colour of machine embroidery thread; set it for straight stitch. Keep the feed dog down when stitching. Using the darning foot, stitch the upper area of the design by building up layers of thread. Try to develop a rhythm between your hand movements and the speed of the machine as this prevents the machine from jamming; this takes practice.*

3 *Continue to fill areas of the design with the first colour of machine embroidery thread. Then rethread the machine with a second colour and stitch more areas of the design in the same way.*

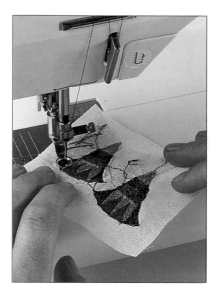

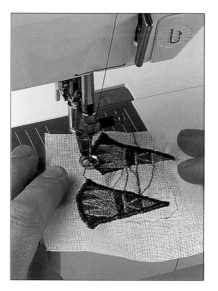

4 Continue to stitch the design using other colours of thread until all the areas of the design have been filled. This design uses only four colours of thread, but they are rich colours which all work well together.

5 Using metallic thread, outline colours within the design by overstitching with a tight zigzag stitch. Then thread the machine with an outline colour and, using a wider zigzag, overstitch the border.

6 Place the stitched muslin face-down on an old towel. Iron the muslin with a very hot iron until it turns a burnt brown colour. Muslin burns at a lower temperature than thread. Leave the muslin to cool.

7 When the muslin has cooled, rub it between your hands and the muslin will flake away, leaving the stitched threads intact. Pull off any remaining pieces of muslin with your fingers and trim loose threads with a pair of sharp scissors.

8 Thread a fine or beading needle with a double thickness of strong cotton in the outline colour. Make a few stitches in the back of one earring to secure the thread, then stitch small beads on to each earring. To finish, make a few stitches in the back of the earring, then snip off the thread.

9 Cut a 3cm (1¼in) length of wire with wire cutters. Insert one end in the top of one earring; loop the end with round-nosed pliers. Thread three beads on to the wire; make a loop with the remaining wire (see inset). Attach the ear wire and secure with pliers; repeat with the second earring.

Kaleidoscope Necklet

MATERIALS

Newsprint
Wallpaper paste
White emulsion paint
Water-based
gouache paints
Oil-based
polyurethane varnish
Whipping cord
Jump ring and clasp
Wooden beads

EQUIPMENT

Cake rack
Artist's brushes
Knitting needles
Small dish
Scissors

ARESPLENDENT EXAMPLE of the wonders that can be achieved at very little cost, this rainbow necklace can be made with the most basic of DIY ingredients – sheets of newspaper and wallpaper paste. Papier mâché is a very amenable material; having made a Matisse-bright necklace, you could try variations. Experiment with cubes, ovals, dangling hearts, or huge beads (modelled around ping-pong balls). Try stringing several strands together for an African-inspired collar, or create a *mille-feuille* of flat circles threaded close together.

The cheapness and easy availability of the materials mean that you can afford to experiment, and ditch your disasters. You could turn out a Christmas choker in holly colours with touches of tinsel, a wedding special in white and gold, or a spectacular Carmen Miranda-style necklace in extrovert fruit shapes. On the other hand, baubles with a smooth finish and subtle colours to match a favourite dress would confer instant sophistication on a shoestring.

Paper Rainbow
*This necklace is
unabashed fun; its
primary colours and
knobbly tactile shapes
have the air of a
Mexican fiesta, and
give a decided lift to
the spirits. Wooden
spacer beads echo the
primary colours.*

Confetti Colours
*Painted paper beads can sport any image you fancy –
stripes, spots, and even faces. Here, newsprint is the background for
muted colour, and metal links give an airy look.*

Making the Beads

Having read the Sunday papers, you can then
tear them to shreds. Forget about the bad news and create
your own pulp fantasy instead.

Wallpaper paste

White
emulsion paint

Newsprint

Water-based
gouache paints

Wooden beads

Bolt ring
and clasp

Oil-based
polyurethane
varnish

Whipping cord

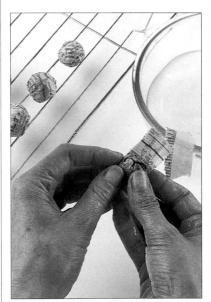

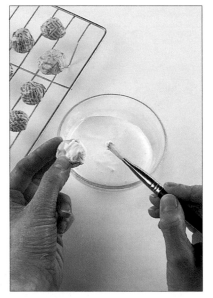

1 *Tear newsprint into small pieces roughly 12.5 x 5cm (5 x 2in). Dip one piece in wallpaper paste, and scrunch it up to make a round ball shape. Cover with smaller pieces of paper and smooth down. Repeat to make a total of 17 shapes, ranging in size, and place them on a cake rack to dry for 48 hours.*

2 *Using an artist's brush, paint each "bead" in turn with a coat of white emulsion paint. This covers the newsprint and provides a plain surface to decorate. Leave the painted paper beads on the cake rack to dry for at least two hours.*

3 *Push four or five of the beads on to a knitting needle, spacing them approximately 2.5cm (1in) apart, to enable you to decorate them on all sides at once.*

4 *Using water-based gouache paint, decorate the beads with a range of multicoloured squiggles, stripes, and dots. Prop the knitting needle over a small dish and leave the beads to dry for two hours.*

5 *Take the dry beads off the needle. Replace one bead at a time on the needle and dip it into a tin of varnish. Flick the excess varnish on to newsprint, then leave the beads to dry on the cake rack for approximately five hours.*

6 *Arrange the beads in the order of threading, with the largest beads in the centre, and the smallest ones at the two ends. Cut a long length of whipping cord. Tie one end of the cord on to the bolt ring, leaving a long end. Starting at one end of the necklace, thread the cord through the beads, alternating paper beads with wooden beads.*

7 *When you have threaded on the last bead, tie the clasp securely on to the end of the cord. Rethread the long end, which was left when attaching the bolt ring, back through a few of the beads to hide it. Trim off the visible end of the cord to neaten.*

Renaissance Riches

MATERIALS

Brightly coloured silk

Hot water
dissolvable fabric

Metallic threads

PVC plastic

Machine
embroidery threads

Coloured
cotton threads

Cardboard

Silk lining

Water

Fine gauze fabric

Velvet

Metallic silk

Variety of beads

Goldwork
metallic pieces

Brass wire,
1mm (¹⁄₁₆ in) thick

Epoxy resin

Hat pin

EQUIPMENT

Scissors

Pins

Sewing machine

Deep-sided dish

Kettle

Needle

Embroidery hoop

Fine sewing scissors

Wire cutters

Round-nosed pliers

THIS INTRICATE HAT PIN, which exploits many techniques and is enriched by sumptuous encrustations of colour and texture, might well have embellished the headband of a Medici beauty. The magical transition from basic raw materials to finished work of art is extraordinary, and relies on the layering of embroidery, fabric, beading, and metal curlicues. The steps are fiddly, but none is very complicated in itself, and the result is refined and ethereal with a subtlety of colour and a fascinating texture that demand closer inspection.

Part of the pleasure of making this hat pin derives from using vanishing muslin as a base; in this case boiling water was used to dissolve the backing fabric (see pp.36–37 where the backing is burned away). This piece is the outcome of much experimentation with different layers and fabrics. Once you have mastered the stages, you could incorporate metallic gauze, lace, or ribbon, and add different beads.

Filigree Stitching
This hat pin, which might easily have graced the feathered cockade of any self-respecting cavalier, is an essential accessory to transform the plain and everyday with a theatrical touch of splendour.

Pin Spectacular
Extra coloured beads, more wire, or added free-falling dangles — these unusually-shaped hat pins can take anything that a magpie imagination can dream up.

Assembling the Hat Pin

*Collect all your bright scraps and silks together,
and try out the effect of different fabrics and colours with
each other. Finish with your most glamorous beads.*

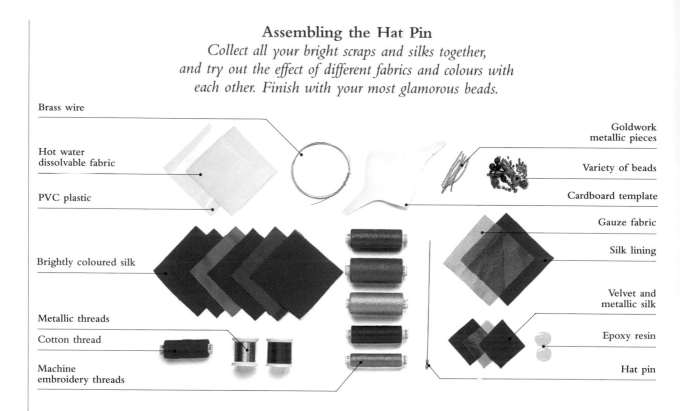

Brass wire

Hot water dissolvable fabric

PVC plastic

Brightly coloured silk

Metallic threads

Cotton thread

Machine embroidery threads

Goldwork metallic pieces

Variety of beads

Cardboard template

Gauze fabric

Silk lining

Velvet and metallic silk

Epoxy resin

Hat pin

1 *Cut out several small squares of brightly coloured silk and lay them out on top of a piece of hot water dissolvable fabric so they cover it entirely. Sprinkle some short lengths of metallic thread over the top. Place a piece of PVC plastic on top of the threads and pin to secure.*

2 *Prepare your sewing machine for free running stitch, threading gold machine embroidery thread in the top, and a contrasting cotton thread in the bobbin. Loosen the bobbin tension. When you begin stitching, the bottom thread should be brought up so that it lies on the surface of the fabric, creating a knobbly effect. Stitch over the PVC plastic in a pattern of loops and squiggles.*

44

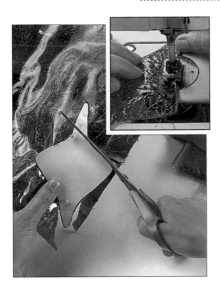

3 Make a cardboard template for the fabric shape. Pin it to the embroidered fabric; cut out the shape. Cut out the same shape from the silk lining. Stitch the embroidered piece to the lining, with the PVC facing outwards. Trim off excess silk. Using metallic and cotton threads, zigzag stitch around the shape (see inset).

4 Lay the embroidered piece in a deep-sided dish. Pour boiling water over the top to submerge the piece. The hot water dissolvable fabric will shrink, making the plastic bubble up. Remove the piece after a few seconds, when it stops moving and shrinking. Rinse in cold water, then squeeze out any excess. Leave to dry.

5 Twist the long ends of the piece and fold them in towards the centre of the design. Pin in position, leaving a section clear for the metal hat pin to be threaded through at the top and bottom, then hand-stitch the ends down to secure.

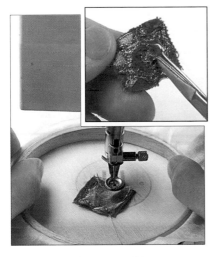

6 Insert a fine gauze fabric in an embroidery hoop. Place a small square of velvet in the hoop, then add a square of silk and two squares of metallic silk on top. Using contrasting metallic threads, stitch a spiral pattern over the squares in free running stitch. Remove the stitched squares from the hoop, then, using fine scissors, cut away some of the silk to reveal the velvet between the stitching (see inset).

7 Stitch the embroidered velvet square to the centre of the main piece, sewing a bead in with each stitch. Then decorate the piece further with a variety of different-shaped beads and goldwork metallic pieces, attaching each of them with a few small stitches.

8 Cut two 9cm (3¾in) lengths of brass wire with wire cutters. Using round-nosed pliers, bend the wires into two small spiral shapes. Stitch these to the back of the piece, so that they protrude at each side. Glue a large bead on to the end of the metal hat pin with epoxy resin. When dry, thread the hat pin through the gaps in the top and bottom of the embroidered piece.

Ideas to Inspire

Paper and fabric jewellery is all about magic. Now you have seen the amazing range of techniques and the fabulous results which can be exacted from these most humble and universally available materials, we show on these pages many more wonders using the same simple elements. Even the most parsimonious would-be jeweller will not begrudge a foray into the fabric scrap-bag or wastepaper basket, and the most cautious surely cannot resist the temptation to experiment, especially when the results can be this spectacular!

▼ Miniature Vegetables
A cauliflower brooch and sprout earrings are made from hand-dyed silk taffeta and organza, glued to a polystyrene base. The centre of the cauliflower is made from tiny beads.

▲ Radical Radishes
Cotton balls dyed with fabric dye were used to make this radish hat pin and earrings. The leaves were made from hand-dyed wired silk, and attached to the radishes by a wired cord stalk. A radish was wired to each ear hook; one was glued to a hat pin.

▶ Heart Beads
These tiny heart earrings are made from red velvet decorated with shiny gold machine embroidery and blue beads.

◀ Dramatic Plastic
Dustbin liners, blue plastic carrier bags, and old crisp packets are recycled to make these striking hand-hooked earrings. The large, floppy loops on the silver earrings give the pieces extra chutzpah.

◀ Silver Lace
These delicate earrings were machine-embroidered with metallic thread on water-soluble dissolvable fabric. The more open, lacy stitches of the star earrings were laminated in plastic for durability.

▲ Paper Triangles
Decorated with a combination of printing techniques, and gold, silver, and copper powders, the paper for these brooches was pieced together to create rich layers of patterning.

▼ Deeply Felt
Made with pre-dyed woollen fleece felted with washing powder, these chunky necklaces will make a brilliant impact on a grey day. The addition of shiny studs (bottom) transforms a couple of stripy felt balls into a pair of earrings.

◀ Literary Links
Inspired by William Shakespeare, these wooden brooches and cufflinks were decorated with découpage from colour photocopies.

► Stitched Silk

These padded and stuffed silk earrings and brooch are embellished with appliqué and rich stitch-work techniques, using shiny rayon threads, to create intricate decoration and intensity of colour.

▲ Tubular Beads

Made with pieces of clear plastic tubing cut to different lengths, this necklace is decorated with coloured threads and strung together with gold silk cord. Some of the pieces of tubing have been scored to create textural indentations.

◄ Paper Discs

To make these earrings, small discs were cut from handmade textured paper, decorated with gouache paint and gold ink, and sealed. The coloured discs were then threaded on to wire along with papier mâché beads.

▼ Paper and Silk

These colourful necklaces combine rolled paper tubes with silks and silver-plated and wooden beads. The tubes were made from screen-printed paper, with added sponged and brushed colour, and copper, silver, and gold powders for extra richness and depth.

► Studded Brooches

Made from tiny pieces of newsprint layered over shaped cardboard, these papier mâché brooches are decorated with pieces of mirror glass, coloured glitter, beads, and gold paint.

▼ Hearts and Stars

Hearts, moons, and stars are popular motifs in jewellery. These earrings are made from papier mâché decorated with flat-backed gemstones and sweet wrappers (below), and paints (right).

► Beaded Stitchery

Created by intricate machine embroidery over vanishing muslin, this stitched pendant is further embellished with tiny copper, gold, and amber beads. The pendant is hung on a wrapped, beaded cord.

▼ Gilded Paper

To create these intriguing pieces, layers of cartridge paper were laminated with PVA glue and decorated with acrylic paints, gilding metals, and creams. The pieces were then scratched and embossed.

Beads and
Glass Jewellery

....

BEADS ARE UNIVERSAL. From pole
to pole, people are busy threading
beads, and all kinds of other things,
on to thongs or threads, slinging
them around their necks, and feeling all the better
for it. Bead-threading is a matter of patience and a
good eye. These projects give you guidelines to
ensure you get good vibrations, not cacophony,
around your neck, down to the last vital detail of
finish and closure. Mirror mosaic, on the other
hand, requires a great leap of imagination in its
design, a steady hand, and a certain amount of
skill to put the pieces together; but the result is so
madly glamorous that it is definitely worth
persevering with the technique. Stained glass
droplets are something of a challenge, but not
really difficult, and the method adapts well to
earrings and circular pendants. Anything that
glisters is as good as gold for the ingenious
jewellery fanatic.

Millefiori Mosaic Beads

MATERIALS
Polymer clay
Seed beads
Gold-plated
jewellery wire

EQUIPMENT
Scalpel
Rolling pin
Needle
Baking tray
Oven
Wire cutters
Round-nosed pliers

POLYMER CLAY is another miracle of modern technology – in addition to being colourful and malleable, it also keeps its shape after a brief baking. If your childhood was spent rolling endless modelling-clay sausages, you will have a head start for this more refined kindergarten pastime, which could well have the same therapeutic effect as kneading bread dough. As you become proficient at the rolling techniques involved, you can then progress to making beads of great delicacy and sophistication.

A limited palette tends to look better than a jazzy motley of brilliant colours. Black and white beads can look smart, as can the earth colours of Aboriginal "dreaming" paintings. Parchment and indigo are also an attractive combination. Making this project is an ideal occasion to enlist the help of young children, but bear in mind that you have to be cautious with the fumes that polymer clay produces on baking – open all the windows for this stage. Some people have discovered that turning up the oven to a really high heat for the final ten minutes or so of baking gives the finished beads a shiny, almost ceramic look.

Fired with Enthusiasm
It takes practice to achieve this deft touch with detail, but the learning experience is a soothing and pleasurable one, and your creations will be entirely original. Be patient, and look at books on mosaics for inspiration.

Wrap and Roll
Once you have mastered the basic techniques of using polymer clay, it is child's play to make a pair of earrings to match your necklace.

52

Making the Beads
*Find a handful of toning colours, flex your
creative muscles, and get to work.*

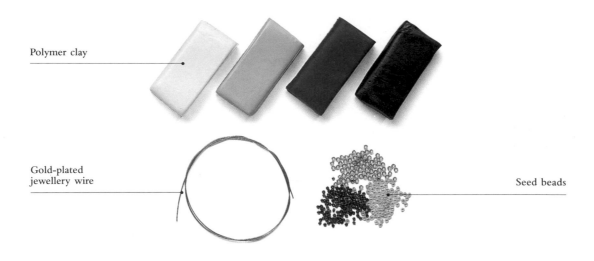

Polymer clay

Gold-plated
jewellery wire

Seed beads

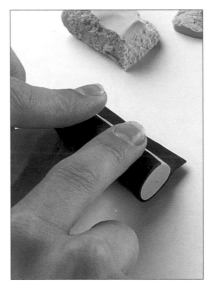

1 *Soften half a block of black
polymer clay by kneading it for
several minutes on a work surface.
Soften half a block of white polymer
clay in the same way. Flatten out a
thin sheet of each colour, roll them
smooth with a rolling pin, then trim
the edges with a scalpel to make
rectangles. Place the white rectangle
on top of the black rectangle, roll them
with a rolling pin to remove any air
bubbles, then carefully roll them up
to form a spiral cane. Set aside.*

2 *To make a wrapped log, knead
a block of first black, then beige,
polymer clay until pliable. Make a log
shape with beige clay. Wrap this log
with a very thin sheet of black clay.
Trim the edges of the black clay where
they meet so the edges butt up exactly
and do not overlap. Roll the wrapped
log gently with your fingers to
consolidate the shape. Set aside.*

3 *Next make a striped log. First
knead a piece each of terracotta,
beige, white, and black polymer clay
separately to soften, then roll each
piece into a square sheet and lay them
one on top of the other. Press down
evenly to consolidate the block and
trim the edges with a scalpel. Cut the
block in half and place one half on top
of the other. Press down evenly again,
thinning out the stripes. Repeat the
process until the stripes are as fine
as required. Set aside.*

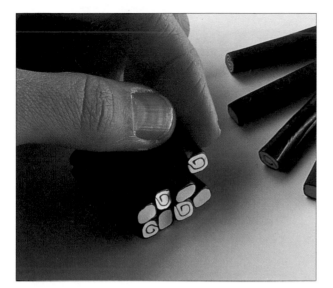

4 To make a chequerboard cane, square the ends of a spiral cane (see step 1) and a wrapped log (see step 2) with your fingers. Elongate the canes by smoothing along each side with your thumb and forefinger. Cut four pieces from each cane and stack them to form a chequerboard pattern. Lengthen this cane by rolling each side evenly.

5 Take the striped block (see step 3) and slice it thickly with a scalpel. Lay these pieces around a piece of the black and white spiral cane, with the stripes running lengthways. Roll this cane to smooth out the seams and reduce its diameter.

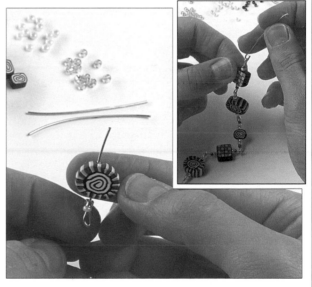

6 Take all the patterned canes and use a scalpel to slice off as many beads as you require for a necklace. Each bead should be at least 5mm (¼in) thick to allow for piercing. Using a needle, pierce each of the beads (see inset). Piercing from one side to the middle, then from the other side to the middle will help to centre the hole. Place the beads on a baking tray and bake at 135°C (265°F/ Gas Mark ¼) for approximately 30–45 minutes.

7 Assemble the necklace by threading polymer clay beads together with seed beads on to gold-plated wire. Cut a 5cm (2in) length of wire with wire cutters. Loop one end of the wire with round-nosed pliers, thread on two seed beads, then one polymer clay bead. Then thread on two more seed beads and make a loop in the top of the wire to secure. Loop the next length of wire through this loop (see inset) and thread on beads as above. Repeat to make the necklace as long as you like. Join up the two ends by looping two adjoining wires.

Stained Glass Pendant

MATERIALS
Paper
Coloured glass
Channelled lead
Glass nugget
Flux
Solder
Bolt ring
Chain

EQUIPMENT
Black felt-tip pen
Glass cutter
Square-nosed pliers
Lead knife
Fid (see p.10)
Soldering iron

NOTHING ELSE has quite the same intense colour as stained glass; it casts a luminous glow whenever the light catches it. You have only to think of cathedral windows tracing a bright rainbow on the nave to appreciate just how sumptuous and special glass can be. Its unique transparency and colour make it a particularly exciting material to use. Once you start to look carefully, you will notice that coloured glass can have differing qualities. Some is smoothly even, and some is ribbed and rippled in a fascinating way. Some familiarity with the glass cutter and the soldering iron might suggest other possibilities. Using mirror glass, for example, adds flashes of light and a sparkle that is irresistible: people always comment on mirror jewellery.

In addition to making brooches, pendants, and earrings, you might stray into the realms of home decoration and experiment with making adornments for light fittings and candlesticks. Before you know it, you will be drawn by glassblowers' and glaziers' waste, and pieces of coloured, pressed, or engraved glass, or even stray chandelier droplets, will become thrilling additions to your repertoire.

Light Fantastic
Like a miniature stained glass window, this glass pendant casts wonderfully colourful shadows. Fortunately, no one has yet thought to put a tax on pure light and colour, so you can indulge in these luxuries extravagantly.

Shapely Shards
You will never tire of simple permutations of shape and colour because of the peculiarly seductive quality of glass. Colour is one of life's greatest pleasures, and glass is colour at its most pure.

Making the Pendant

*Experiment with your soldering iron until you feel
familiar with it, and can control the magical transformation
of dull metal by burnishing with heat.*

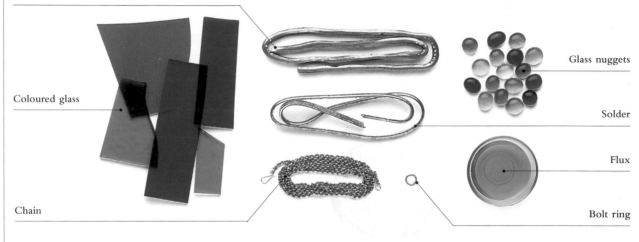

Channelled lead

Glass nuggets

Coloured glass

Solder

Flux

Chain

Bolt ring

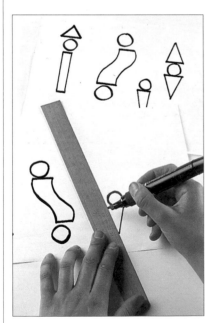

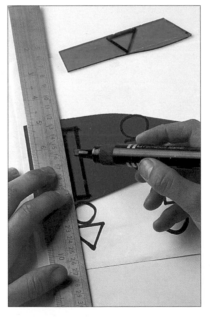

1 *Using a black felt-tip pen and
a ruler, draw out a design for
your pendant on paper. Keep to
simple, bold shapes, such as triangles,
rectangles, and diamonds, as these are
easier to cut out of glass. Circles are
difficult to cut from a piece of glass,
but you can use glass nuggets instead.*

2 *Decide on the colours of glass
you want to use for each element
of the pendant. Then lay a piece of
coloured glass over each of the drawn
shapes in turn, and trace the shapes
on to the glass using a black felt-tip
pen and a ruler.*

3 *Cut out the shapes drawn on
the glass using a glass cutter. Cut
either inside or outside the pen outline
consistently for all pieces. Holding the
glass cutter upright, push it away from
you, keeping your hand steady. Once
you have started cutting along a line
do not stop until you reach the end,
because the glass could splinter off
resulting in an uneven edge.*

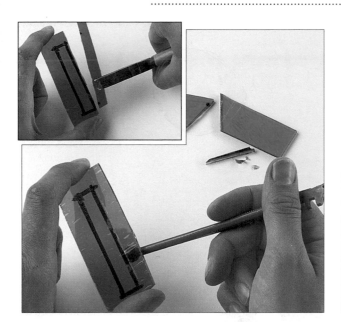

4 *Once you have cut around the drawn shape, tap gently on the underside of the glass along the scored line, with the ball of the glass cutter. Holding the glass firmly in one hand, use square-nosed pliers to grip the glass close to the scored line and pull it away. The glass should break in one piece and come away in the pliers (see inset). If it does not break off, repeat the tapping and pulling. Cut out all the pieces for the pendant in the same way*

5 *Take a length of channelled lead and wrap it around each of the glass sections of the pendant in turn, including the glass nugget. Channelled lead is quite flexible and will wrap easily. Cut off the spare lead using a lead knife. As lead is quite soft, cutting it is rather like cutting through cheese. To secure the glass, press the lead into the sides of the glass using a fid (see inset). Repeat with all sections of the pendant.*

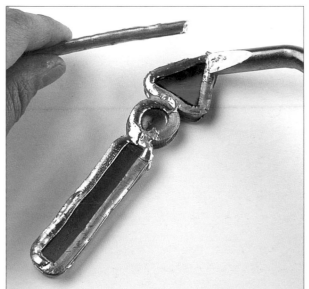

6 *Solder the sections of the pendant together. To do this, first apply flux on the joins with a paintbrush, then solder with a soldering iron following the manufacturer's instructions. Hold the stick of solder on the join, then touch this with the soldering iron. The solder will melt into the joins, securing the pieces together.*

7 *Run the solder around the lead to give it a silver appearance. Then solder a bolt ring on the end of, and at right angles to, the pendant. Leave the pendant to cool, then wash it in washing-up liquid to remove the flux. Rinse and leave to dry. Finally, thread a chain through the bolt ring to complete the pendant.*

Four-stranded Necklace

MATERIALS
Silver-plated
jewellery wire
Very fine fuse wire
Assorted beads
Black polyester thread
Superglue

EQUIPMENT
Wire cutters
Round-nosed pliers
Scissors
Needle

THERE IS A FINE ART to putting beads together. To the uninitiated it may seem that a necklace virtually assembles itself, but, when you get down to it, you will find that the beads you thought were destined for a long and harmonious relationship do not do anything for each other at all, and those you wanted to ditch are perfect partners for your beloved favourites. There are some magnificent bead catalogues available which make the whole process of choosing beads rather less fraught, though nothing really beats feeling, weighing, seeing, and trying one particular bead with another.

Colours and quantities are just a matter of taste and experience but, to start with, it is comforting to have some guidance. If your beads look good in a heap, they will look good when threaded together; in this instance, there is a cohesive common denominator of colour and material. Glass beads tend to be the most expensive, but they also have an enduring shine and inimitable glowing transparency.

Threaded Treasure
This sophisticated, dressy necklace is coloured with shades of glowing berry reds, marbled with black, and given a touch of silver. Different beads give very different looks; shiny glass, faceted crystal, or glinting metal are all sophisticated, while matt glass, dark antiqued metal, dull brass or copper, and wood are more casual.

Venerable Beads
These necklaces both have beads of roughly similar scale and colour for a balanced effect.

60

Threading the Beads
Choose beads in a limited range of colours, and
add a touch of contrast in silver or gold.

Black polyester thread

Silver-plated jewellery wire

Assorted beads

Very fine fuse wire

Superglue

1 *Using wire cutters, cut a piece of silver-plated jewellery wire about 6cm (2½in) long. Using round-nosed pliers, make a small loop in the wire, then coil the rest of the wire at right angles to the loop to make a tight coil. Repeat the process to make another 11 wire coils. Set aside.*

2 *Cut a piece of very fine fuse wire about 6–8cm (2½–3¼in) long. Make a tiny loop at one end with round-nosed pliers. Thread three or four small beads on to the wire. Then, using the pliers, fold the top of the wire back on itself to secure the beads. Repeat the process to make another seven beaded pieces.*

3 *Cut four strands of black polyester thread, each approximately 1m (40in) long. Thread assorted beads on to the first strand, starting with a large decorative bead in the centre. Make the strands of beads symmetrical and choose beads in complementary colours. Leave approximately 30cm (12in) thread at each end.*

4 *Thread the other three strands with beads in a similar way, keeping the same colour palette for all four strands and ensuring that all the strands look good together. Intersperse the wire coils and beaded pieces (see steps 1 and 2) among the beads. Leave roughly 28.5cm (11½in) of thread at each end.*

5 *Tie a 2m (80in) length of black polyester thread in a knot around the four threads at one end of the beaded strands. You should now have six trailing ends of thread. Thread all six strands of thread into a 5mm (¼in) bead and push the bead up against the knot. Repeat this process with the four threads at the other end of the necklace.*

6 *Divide the six threads at one end into three sections: a middle section consisting of the four original threads, and two longer threads, one on each side. To braid, take the left-hand thread under the middle threads, and over the right-hand thread. Then take the right-hand thread over the middle threads and under the left-hand thread. Repeat down the length of the threads.*

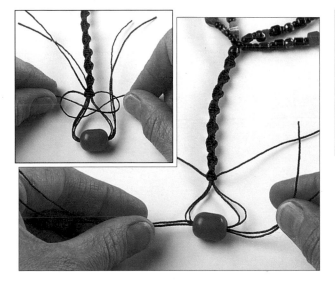

7 *Braid to within 2cm (¾in) of the end of the threads. The braiding will twist and tighten as you go. Then split the four middle threads into two and thread them through a large bead, with two threads going into the bead from one side, and the other two from the other side. Bring the thread ends back up towards the braiding and tie the longer outer threads over them to secure (see inset). Braid the outer threads over the middle thread ends to neaten.*

8 *Repeat step 6 with the other end of the necklace. Then plait the middle threads to make a button hole large enough to fit over the bead (see step 7). Fold the plaited threads back to the braiding to create a loop, tie the outer threads over the ends to secure, then braid the outer threads over the ends to neaten. Thread the ends through the braiding three times with a needle to neaten (see inset). Trim the ends, then dab them with superglue to secure.*

Glittering Regalia

MATERIALS

Paper
Coloured mirror glass
Flat-backed
glass rhinestones
Aluminium foil
Fibre-glass resin
Thin gauge wire
Brooch pin
Bolt rings
Water

EQUIPMENT

Pen
Glass cutter
Long-nosed pliers
Snips
Protective mask
Small container
Cocktail stick
Scalpel
Adhesive putty
Wire cutters
Toothbrush

THIS IS THEATRICAL glamour *par excellence* and perfect for your own personal coronation, to commemorate some particularly daring exploit of an amatory or ambitious nature, or just for the 18-carat fun of it. This brooch is not for those who feel perfectly happy in a single strand of carefully graduated freshwater pearls – this is a showy, glorious celebration of the joy of kitsch. It contains all the elements of a jeweller's repertoire of significant and seductive motifs – hearts, diamonds, teardrops, stars, crescents, and crosses – expressed in a royal ransom of chunks of glittering mirror glass.

It is all too often forgotten, in the curious human urge to flaunt its fortune, that jewellery is as much about fun and theatre as it is about money, if not more so. This flamboyant piece takes a humorous and ironic over-the-top angle on the whole matter of self-adornment. If you ever yearned to break the ice at parties, you will find that this is the decoration to do it. This brooch can be medal of honour for the shy or a badge of predictable victory for the extrovert.

Royal Flush
A study in scarlet and black, this elegantly bedizened brooch is to be worn with chutzpah and a broad smile. Alternatively, having mastered the intricacies of the mosaic brooch, you could treat the waiting world to a mosaic-spangled tiara.

Mirror Image
This brooch, made of faceted reflective mirror, sparkles with the same coruscations as the glittering gems that dazzle the eye at society galas, but without the cost.

Making the Brooch

Enjoy the enormous range of finishes and
colours that is the province of glass alone, but treat glass
respectfully, since it can inflict injury.

Aluminium foil

Paper

Fibre-glass resin

Coloured mirror glass

Flat-backed glass rhinestones

Plain mirror glass

Brooch pin

Bolt rings

Thin gauge wire

1 Draw a life-sized design for your brooch on paper. Using a glass cutter (see steps 3–4 on pp.58–59), cut coloured mirror glass into strips. Then use long-nosed pliers and snips to break up the strips of mirror glass into smaller pieces.

2 Assemble the pieces of glass, together with the flat-backed glass rhinestones, on top of the drawn design on the paper. Laying out the pieces on paper first allows you to change colours and adjust shapes as you go. Working on one part of the brooch at a time, transfer the mosaic pieces on to a square of aluminium foil. Position them carefully, following the initial design.

3 Work in a well-ventilated room and wear a protective mask as the fumes are quite strong. Mix fibre-glass resin in a small container using a cocktail stick. Dribble the resin around the mosaic edges with the cocktail stick. The resin will run underneath the glass pieces to form a pool on the aluminium foil. Keep teasing the pieces together with the cocktail stick.

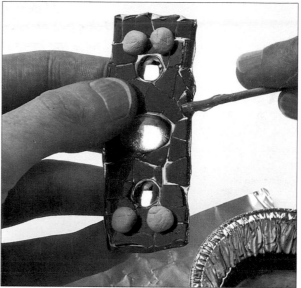

4 The resin will take about 8 minutes to dry. Keep testing the edges. When it feels like thick jelly it is ready. Using a scalpel, cut around the edge of the brooch through the aluminium foil. Wait another few minutes for the resin to harden, then peel the foil off the back.

5 Stick adhesive putty on the front of the brooch (this will keep it raised off the surface when you lay it down). Using a cocktail stick, apply liquid resin around the edges of the brooch. Place the brooch face-down on the aluminium foil so that you can work on the back of it.

6 Coat the back of the brooch with liquid resin. Then, using wire cutters, cut four pieces of wire, 2cm (¾in) long, and bend these into loops with pliers. Lay these wire loops along one long edge of the brooch bar, so that the loops overhang the edge. Apply another coat of liquid resin over the wire loops to secure them in place. Position a brooch pin in the centre of the brooch, on the opposite side to the loops. Seal with another coat of liquid resin (see inset) then, when dry, apply a further coat.

7 Make the brooch charms in the same way as the brooch bar, attaching wire loops to the top then bolt rings to the loops to link the pieces. Open out the bolt rings with long-nosed pliers and hook each one through a wire loop in the brooch bar to assemble the brooch. Squeeze the rings to close. Clean the front of the brooch by first dampening it with water, then scraping off any excess resin with a scalpel. Finally, scrub the front of the brooch with a toothbrush to remove any remaining traces of resin.

Ideas to Inspire

Having dabbled with kindergarten materials such as paper, you may now wish to venture into more glamorous territory — .glass and beads are your natural allies. This is the magpie realm of glitz and kitsch, and all the more exciting for its heady mixture of sparkle and ingenuity. Take inspiration from the following pages and be bold, brash, and brassy. There is every reason to have fun with wild and wonderful creations: the glitterati show the way!

▼ Square Blocks
Polymer clay is the basis for these striking square earrings. The pattern was built up using seven colours of clay; then the squares were sliced off the block.

◄ Sparkling Stars
Shards of mirror and smaller fragments of red glass were arranged together to form this dramatic star-shaped brooch and matching earrings. The glass is held together with a backing of several coats of resin.

▶ Indian Inspiration
Based on Indian motifs, these brooches were constructed from modelling clay built up in layers on cardboard shapes. Silver balls and beads, and tiny pieces of mirror were inserted into the clay to add sparkle. Finally the clay was painted.

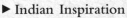

▼ **Kitsch Cuffs**

These chunky bracelets are made from a base of twisted copper wire, through which strands of tiny coloured beads are woven and secured with wire. Larger beads of glass, ceramic, plastic, and paper are interspersed throughout the pieces for added colour and drama.

▶ **Diamanté Necklaces**

These glittering pendants are cast in plastic from moulds in the shape of crosses, hearts, and stars. Holes are drilled in the plastic, and diamanté inserted and glued to secure. Fine silver chains complete the pieces.

▲ **Beaded Knuckledusters**

These silver rings are decorated with exuberant clusters of plastic beads and sparkling coloured glass, threaded on to a silver wire base, which is then securely attached to the ring.

▶ **Planetary Influences**

Pieces of plain and coloured mirror glass were cut with snips and arranged to create these dazzling designs, held together with layers of resin. Brooch pins were embedded in the final layer.

◄ Thonged Beads
Simplicity works: a handful of natural-coloured, stone-washed glass beads are threaded on to a fine leather thong. Knots tied in the leather between the beads hold them robustly in place.

◄ Threaded Pebbles
These necklaces are made using only natural materials. Pebbles are notched with a file, or a small hole is drilled at each side; then they are knotted together with waxed flax. Wooden beads give a contrast of texture.

◄ Sunburst Brooch
The centre of this brooch is a seashell, on to which are soldered even-sized shards of mirror glass, to represent a sunburst. The glass rays are also soldered, to cover any sharp edges.

▼ Pipe Pieces

Inspired by native American jewellery, these necklaces are made from pieces of broken clay pipe threaded on string. Uncut semi-precious stones and a variety of small feathers were assembled together with silver wire to make up the pendants, creating the impression of little ziggurats.

◄ Moody Colours

Whether you make up your own beads or buy them ready-made, polymer clay is a dream for creating simple necklaces. Use black and white for a sharp, crisp effect (above) or earthy tones (left) for warmth.

Wood and Metal Jewellery

······································

WOOD AND METAL make more durable pieces of jewellery, some of which require a modicum of skill, and somewhat pricier equipment. Don't be daunted – you will, with a bit of practice, be making things that sell for real money. You can carve softwood quite easily, or buy wooden bangles ready made, upon which to paint patterns and sprinkle "gems". You can make formal brooches by miniaturizing picture frames, decorating the tiny strips of wood with paint and gilding. You can also experiment with painted tin; all you need are tin snips, enamel paint, glue, and brooch pins. If you are feeling very ambitious, you could tackle our final project, which requires a certain skill but is manageable for anyone with deft fingers and the necessary tools.

Copper Leaf Brooch

MATERIALS

Picture framing glass,
2mm (⅛in) thick
Sheet copper
Acrylic paints
Pressed leaf
PVA glue
Copper tape
Solder
Washing-up liquid
Water
Superglue
Brooch pin

EQUIPMENT

Metal ruler
Black felt-tip pen
Glass cutter
Scissors
Wire wool
2 artist's brushes
Soft cloth
Soldering iron

THIS PROFESSIONAL-LOOKING brooch makes an evocative country memento. It is easy to produce, using glass, copper tape, and an autumn leaf collected on a frosty morning walk and pressed between the pages of a telephone directory. This particular leaf is from a gingko tree, but the fine leaves of aspen, maidenhair fern, rowan, or decorative acers would all look equally good.

You could adapt this method – which illustrates in effect how to make a tiny picture frame – to show off other favourite souvenirs: a pressed flower, scraps of lace, and ribbon to recollect a wedding; or a stamp, a graphic motif taken from the label of a particularly splendid bottle of wine, contour lines torn from a map, and the hamlet name to remember a holiday in France. Alternatively, if all this effort seems too twee or fussy, you might find an image ready cut in a sheet of scraps, or a perfectly beautiful shell print in a moth-eaten junk-shop book on natural history. The point is that the autumn leaf is charming, and a pun is always fun, but anything flat and tiny will be shown off to advantage in its own miniature copper frame on a background of painted copper leaf.

Grace from Fall
Nature works hard to create beautiful things, and who are we to ignore them? Leaves make wonderful abstract works of art, come in a myriad shapes and colours, cost nothing, and look ravishing in the right setting, as in this stylish brooch.

Well Pressed
These four leaves, carefully pressed and meticulously decorated, are set against painted backgrounds which have a mysterious glow imparted by the copper leaf subtly illuminating the colour.

Assembling the Brooch

*Having pressed your leaf, think carefully about the
colour of paint to use; red and green are boldly complementary,
while yellow glows well against black.*

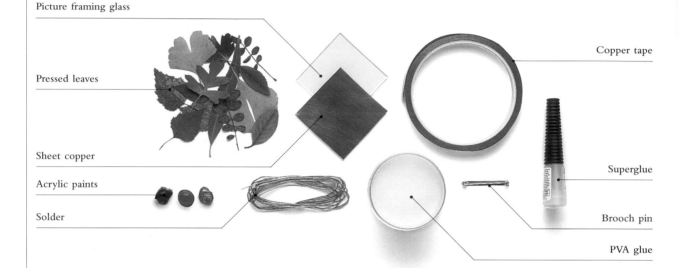

Picture framing glass

Pressed leaves

Sheet copper

Acrylic paints

Solder

Copper tape

Superglue

Brooch pin

PVA glue

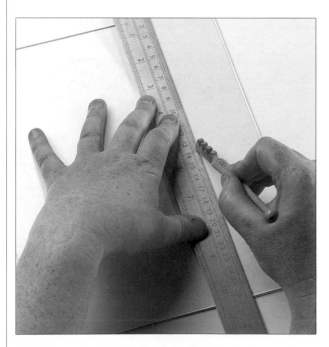

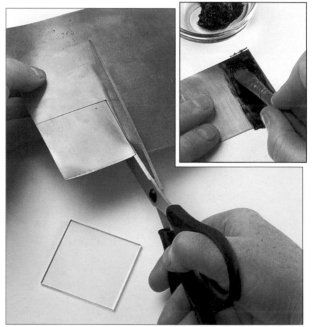

1 Take a piece of picture framing glass and measure
5cm (2in) in from one side at the top and bottom of
the piece. Mark with a felt-tip pen. Place a metal ruler
between the two pen marks, then, holding it with one
hand, cut along the edge of the ruler with a glass cutter
(see steps 3–4 on pp.58–59). Then cut a 5cm (2in)
square from the glass strip in the same way.

2 Place the glass square on a piece of sheet copper.
Draw around the edge with a black felt-tip pen.
Cut out the marked square with scissors. Rub the copper
square with wire wool to give it a slight key for paint to
adhere to. Paint two or three coats of black acrylic paint
over the square (see inset), allowing each coat to dry
before applying the next, and leave to dry.

3 Select a nicely shaped pressed leaf that will fit within the black painted square. Decorate the leaf with gold and red acrylic paint using an artist's brush. Here, the leaf has been decorated with spots of colour, but you can choose any pattern you like. Leave to dry for 5–10 minutes.

4 To assemble the brooch, use PVA glue to stick the decorated leaf centrally on to the black square and leave to dry. Then polish the glass square with a soft cloth and place it on top of the leaf. Cut a length of copper tape to fit around the edges of the square. Peel the sticky layer off the tape and roll the square down the middle of the tape. Fold the copper tape down flat over the edges of the glass and mitre the corners for a neat finish (see inset).

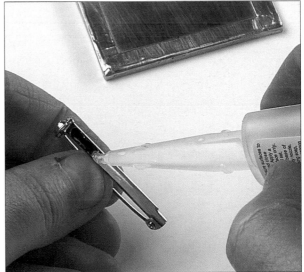

5 Using solder and a soldering iron, solder over the copper tape edging, following the manufacturer's instructions. The solder turns the copper silver and makes the brooch waterproof and durable. Rub the soldered edges and the back of the brooch with wire wool dipped in a drop of washing-up liquid and a tiny amount of water to tone down the shine. Dry thoroughly.

6 To complete the brooch, apply superglue to a brooch pin and position this centrally and horizontally on the upper back of the brooch. Allow the glue to dry for at least an hour before wearing the brooch.

Painted Tin Brooch

MATERIALS

Paper
Sheet steel
Brooch pin
White matt
primer spray paint
Enamel paints

EQUIPMENT

Pen
Tin snips
Block of wood
Metal file
Wet and dry paper
Spot welder
Block of lead
Round-ended
hammer
Artist's brush

SHEET STEEL IS WONDERFULLY EASY to obtain. Making this brooch is a decorative way to recycle bean tins. A spot welder, on the other hand, is something that not everyone can get hold of or use with confidence. If this is your quandary, it is definitely worth experimenting with superglue for a small project such as this brooch.

Painted tin has a glossy slickness that makes it the perfect material for jokey, fun jewellery: you can paint any motif you fancy on it and you can make your brooch any shape you like, adding extra layers or fine detail as you wish, drawing inspiration from anything from comic books to medieval banners. If you are lucky enough to find tins printed with graphics or images that appeal, you can cut them out and use them as they come, or with witty additions of your own. Here, the designer has come up with a strong shape, which she has emphasized with bold primary colours. This is probably the most effective approach to humorous jewellery, but you might experiment with a subtle touch of verdigris or even rust. If you just don't feel dressed without a bit of sparkle, you could always wire a few beads or stick a few gems on to your creation. With junk jewellery, there is no excuse not to have fun.

Star and Stripes
You may never get to be sheriff, but this sassy badge is the perfect partner for favourite faded denims, and has a real transatlantic energy to it.

Steelworks
Enamel paints have an irresistible shine to them and, simply by changing the colours, and adding spots and stripes, you can create infinite variations on a theme of steel. Substituting a crescent moon for the heart varies the design even more.

Assembling the Brooch

Cutting a hollow circle from steel is just about impossible, but by making it in three sections you get the same effect with an interesting layered look.

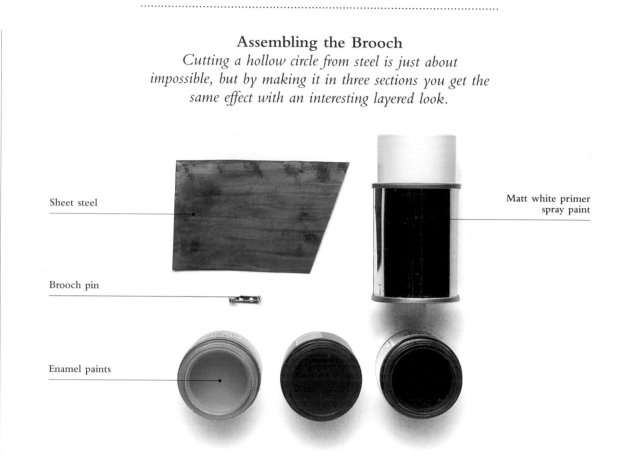

Sheet steel

Matt white primer spray paint

Brooch pin

Enamel paints

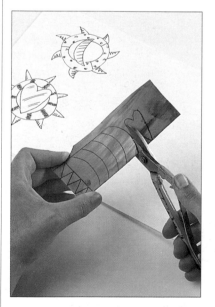

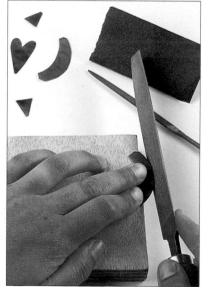

1 *Sketch the design for your brooch on a piece of paper. Then draw all the components of the design on to a piece of sheet steel. Carefully cut out all the pieces using tin snips.*

2 *Take each piece of steel in turn, place it on a block of wood and, holding it down, rub all the edges with a file to smooth. Then sand all the edges with wet and dry paper.*

3 *Using a spot welder, weld the three curved pieces of steel together to form a basic circular shape. Trim the edges with tin snips to neaten the circle.*

4 *Shape the metal heart and circle by holding them in turn over a block of lead, then beating them lightly with a round-ended hammer. This gives the shapes a three-dimensional effect, making the brooch slightly convex in appearance when pinned on to clothing.*

5 *Weld the heart on to the basic circle at the three outermost points. Then weld on the five spikes around the edge of the circle. Turn the brooch over and weld a brooch pin centrally and horizontally on to the upper back of the heart (see inset).*

6 *Working in a well-ventilated area, spray the metal brooch with a coat of white matt primer to create a good surface to paint on. Allow the paint to dry thoroughly, then, using enamel paints, paint the heart red, the circle yellow and the spikes blue. Allow the colours to merge together for a subtle effect.*

7 *Allow the initial paint colours to dry, then paint thin blue stripes around the yellow circle for extra decoration. Leave the brooch to dry thoroughly before wearing it. There is no need to varnish the brooch as the enamel paints provide a high gloss coating and seal the metal against rust very effectively.*

Mixed Media Brooch

MATERIALS

Paper
Metallic silk
Coloured silk
Machine embroidery
threads
Sheet brass,
0.7mm (¹⁄₃₂in) thick
Balsa wood, 2mm
(¹⁄₈in) thick
Water-based ink
Sticky tape
Brooch pin
Wire, 1mm
(¹⁄₁₆in) thick
Double-sided tape
4 brass circles

EQUIPMENT

Pen
Pins
Embroidery hoop
Sewing machine and
darning foot
Scissors
Block of wood
Clamp
Piercing saw
Metal file
Hobby drill and
1mm (¹⁄₁₆in) drill bit
Sandpaper
Artist's brush
Wire cutters
Hammer
Anvil

I F YOU HAVE EVER PLAYED with a doll's house, you will know the fascination of miniature objects. This stitched brooch is, in effect, a tiny framed work of art; with nimble-fingered perseverance you could aspire to a whole gallery for your lapel. But, to look good, tiny things require a meticulous finish - the smaller an object is, the more conspicuous are its defects to the inevitable close inspection. So, when you are making this embroidered brooch, go slowly, take care with each of the stages, and the final result will be a fascinating and unique piece of art.

Machine embroidery is quick, easy, and can draw on the dazzling spectrum of colours to be found wherever needles and pins are sold. A Piscean pair of unknown species adorns this brooch, but you could use any simple, bold, and colourful motif – a summer strawberry, a Valentine heart, a starfish, your initials, a bluebird – that strikes you as being meaningful or pretty. There is no reason why you should not change the size or shape of your brooch, bearing in mind that straight edges are easier to cut with a piercing saw, or embellish its diminutive frame with light-catching studs or tiny copper nail-heads. Instead of painting your miniature wooden frame with coloured ink, you might run to a square of gold leaf or gold antiquing wax to enrich and decorate it.

Fantastic Fish
Bright primary colours and an arresting and appealing image combine to make the recipe for these fish in stitches. The stitching gives a shiny relief texture to the fish and background, almost like scales and water.

Metal Petals
Glowing satin-smooth stitches make the heart of these brooches – they can pulsate with an entire rainbow of threads, or radiate calm with a trio of subtle and mutually flattering colours.

Assembling the Brooch

*Making this brooch will require a little patience;
stitching and sawing may take practice, but you could always
cheat with the brooch pin and stick it on with glue.*

Paper

Silk

Metallic silk

Machine
embroidery
threads

Sheet brass

Balsa wood

Water-based ink

Double-sided tape

Wire, 1mm
(1/16 in) thick

Brass circles

Brooch pin

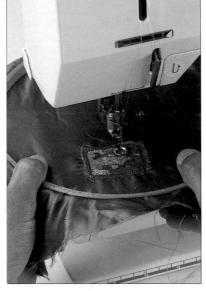

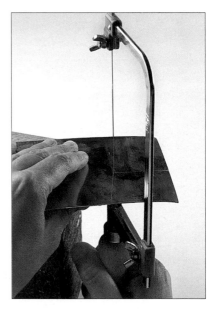

1 *Sketch out the design for your brooch on a piece of paper. Here the design is of a fish but you could choose any motif you like, although simple, easily recognized motifs generally work better at this scale. Pin a small rectangle of metallic silk to a larger piece of silk. Put this in an embroidery hoop.*

2 *Set the sewing machine for straight stitch and thread it with machine embroidery thread. Keeping the feed dog down, and using the darning foot, stitch your brooch design on the silk rectangle. Fill in the design with stitching in different colours of thread so that the entire design is filled with stitching. Cut out the rectangle and set aside.*

3 *Attach a block of wood to a work surface using a clamp. With one hand, hold a piece of sheet brass on the wood so that the end protrudes over the edge of the wood. With the other hand, cut out a rectangle from the brass using a piercing saw. The rectangle should be slightly larger than the embroidered silk rectangle. Smooth the rough edges with a file.*

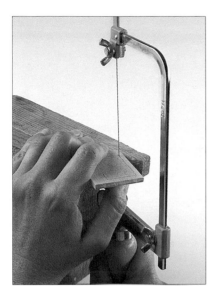

4 Using the piercing saw, cut out a rectangle of wood that is the same size as the sheet brass. Drill a hole in the centre of the wood with a small hobby drill, then insert the piercing saw through the hole and cut out the centre of the wood to make a frame. Rub the edges with sandpaper.

5 Using an artist's brush, paint the wooden frame on both the front and back with a coat of water-based ink to stain it. Then set the frame aside to dry for at least 30 minutes.

6 Tape the brooch pin to the upper centre of the brass rectangle. Place the brass on to a block of wood; drill two holes in the brooch pin. Insert a 2mm (⅛in) length of wire into each hole. Hammer the wires on both sides of the brass; the ends will splay out to rivet the brooch pin to the brass.

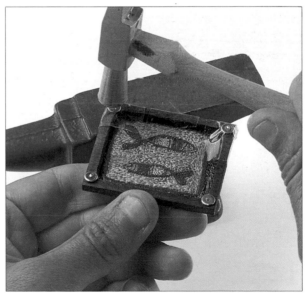

7 Turn the brass rectangle over so that the brooch pin is on the underside, then stick two pieces of double-sided tape on to the brass. Trim any loose threads on the embroidered silk rectangle, then stick it down carefully on the brass, ensuring that the edges of the embroidered silk do not protrude over the brass rectangle.

8 Place the wooden frame over the embroidery and drill a hole through each corner. Tape a brass circle on each corner. Then, holding the brooch over an anvil, hammer a 2mm (⅛in) length of wire through each brass circle and through the layers of the brooch; the wire ends will splay out to rivet the layers together. Remove the tape. Hammer the wire ends on the back of the brooch to secure.

Etched Metal Earrings

MATERIALS
Graph paper
Tracing paper
Sheet brass
Sticky tape
Sheet steel
Printer's stop out
White spirit
Nitric acid (available from chemists)
Water
Pumice powder
Flux
Solder
Earring findings
Silver tubing, 2mm (⅛in) thick

EQUIPMENT
Pen
Scissors
Scriber
Block of wood
Piercing saw
Metal files
Artist's brush
Rubber gloves
Apron
Goggles
Small lidded dish
Soft brush
Brass brush
Tweezers
Blow torch
Drill and 1mm (¹⁄₁₆in) drill bit
Centre punch
Hammer
Glass brush
Soft cloth

THE STARTING POINT for these intricate earrings is pressing your nose up against the glass in a museum of heraldry and armour. There you can search for the most doughty shape of crest or shield to take as your basic outline. You could even plagiarize the odd motif too, or you might simply reproduce the etched heraldic earrings shown here, which could hardly be bettered.

This is one of the more demanding projects in the book and could be described as professional jewellery. You will have to approach it with caution, as some of the processes are tricky and potentially dangerous, but the raw materials are not costly and making the earrings will make an impressive foray into those rarefied realms beyond shiny baubles. Fortunately, as with most things medieval, symmetry is optional; if both earrings do not match exactly, that is very much part of the charm of making your own jewellery. Anyone can buy machine-made bijoux, perfect and matching but lacking soul or character. These earrings, however, evoke the distant echoes of bugles, royal banners, and legendary monarchs, and are all the better for their individual quirks. You could, to start with, fashion a simplified shape based on a shield, and work up to elaborate coronet shapes. Having made a pair of earrings, a brooch will be child's play.

Heraldic Devices
Of course, no one would dream of wearing another's coat of arms, but there is nothing to stop you experimenting with some of the bold charges, devices, and blazoning of medieval heraldry.

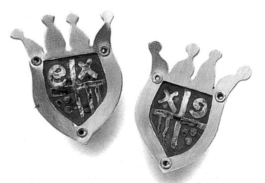

Copper and Steel
The same earrings, but this time made from sheet steel and copper, have a subtler and more discreet effect. Try combining different metals, such as gold and silver, for total glamour.

Making the Earrings

*Making these earrings requires dexterity, as well
as a cool head when using nitric acid and a blow torch.
However, success is something truly to be proud of.*

Silver tubing

Graph paper

Sheet steel

Sheet brass

Earring findings

Printer's stop out

Nitric acid

Flux

Pumice powder

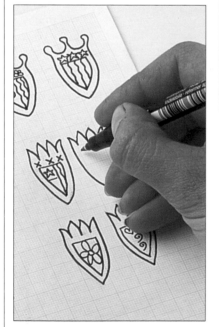

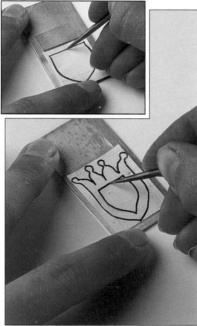

1 *Sketch designs for your earrings on a piece of graph paper to ensure they are symmetrical. These earrings will be composed of two types of metal riveted together so you need to split your design into two layers, one for the earring framework, and the other for the centre. Trace over the two parts of your design on to a sheet of tracing paper and cut them out.*

2 *To make one earring, stick the tracing for the framework of the design on to a piece of sheet brass with sticky tape. Using a scriber, score over the design lines on the tracing. This will transfer the design to the metal beneath. Then stick the tracing for the centre of the design over a piece of sheet steel and repeat the scoring with that design (see inset).*

3 *Holding the scored brass and steel in turn on a block of wood, saw along the scored lines of the earring design with a piercing saw to cut out the two parts of the earring. File all the edges of both pieces with a metal file, using a small file for more intricately-shaped edges (see inset).*

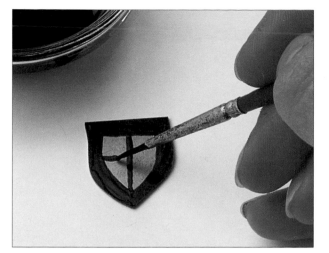

4 Using an artist's brush, paint printer's stop out on the back of the steel, around the edges, and on the front in a simple design. (The printer's stop out should be runny; if it feels too thick, you can thin it down with a little white spirit.) The metal that is covered with the printer's stop out will not be etched out in the next step. Allow the steel piece to dry for approximately 30 minutes.

5 Work in a well-ventilated area to avoid inhaling toxic fumes and wear rubber gloves, apron, and goggles. Add 1 part nitric acid to 5 parts water in a dish and mix well. Put the steel in the dish and cover. When bubbles appear on the steel, brush them away gently with a soft brush. Cover and leave the steel; repeat the brushing every 10 minutes. In 30 minutes the acid will etch out the metal that has not been covered with printer's stop out.

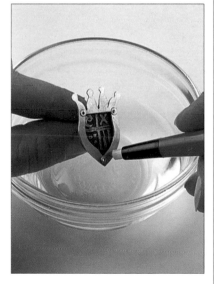

6 Remove the steel from the dish, rinse in cold water, and brush off the printer's stop out using a brass brush dipped in pumice powder and water. To attach the earring finding to the back of the steel, apply flux and solder to the metal. Using tweezers, hold the earring finding in position on the solder and heat the solder with a blow torch to fuse the finding in place.

7 Place the steel piece of the earring behind the brass piece and rivet the two together. To do this, drill a hole in each of the three corners. Insert a 2mm (⅛in) length of silver tubing into each drilled hole in turn, insert a centre punch into the tubing to open up the end, and hammer the centre punch to flatten the tubing to secure. Repeat on both sides of the earring.

8 Clean the earring for maximum shine using a glass brush and water. Then wipe it with a soft cloth for a final polish. Repeat steps 2 to 8 to make a matching earring. When you have completed the earrings, clean all brushes with white spirit.

Ideas to Inspire

Wood and metal are both reassuringly solid materials with character and attraction. There is plenty of inspiration here to satisfy the most discerning eye, and plenty to keep occupied the most adept hand, and ingenuity enough to reveal marvels where before you had only junk. A trip to your local hardware shop – all those shiny chains, washers, wires, and assorted metallica – will make you faint with excitement. So get welding!

▼ Chain Reaction
These delicate steel wire rectangles were easily formed and looped together with pliers to make a necklace. A cut-out silver pendant, based on ancient Indian architecture, hangs from one of the links.

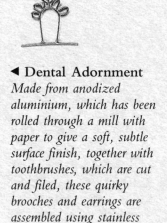

▶ Miniature Gallery
These tiny works of art are executed on sheet copper using a variety of paint techniques to create textural, metallic patterns. The pieces are then covered with picture framing glass and framed with copper tape, which is soldered to give a silvery finish. A brooch pin is glued on to the back.

◀ Dental Adornment
Made from anodized aluminium, which has been rolled through a mill with paper to give a soft, subtle surface finish, together with toothbrushes, which are cut and filed, these quirky brooches and earrings are assembled using stainless steel pins and silver rivets.

▲ Wire Knitting
Copper-coloured wire and shimmering purple thread are knitted together to create these horn-shaped earrings, using four needles to give hollow centres.

▶ **Riveting Silk**
Tiny snippets of machine-embroidered silk are here sandwiched between sheet brass and picture framing glass, and held in position with brass rivets or screws in each corner. Brooch pins are riveted to the backs.

▶ **Fishy Finery**
These inventive brooches are made entirely from recycled materials. The two large fish are made from sheet steel, which is etched with wax and sulphuric acid; the baby fish are made from plastic and enamelled steel, then attached with laminated mesh.

◀ **Beaded Hat Pins**
Simple yet stylish, these hat pins are decorated with a combination of coloured and silver beads, which are glued in place with superglue.

◄ Baroque Pins

Intricate machine embroidery, backed by sunbursts of sheet brass and further embellished with beads and golden curlicues, decorates this duo of resplendent hat pins.

▼ Welded Steel

These pewterish brooches are made from pieces of sheet steel welded together, then given light-catching texture using a hammer and centre punch.

▼ Live Wire

Coloured glass and plastic beads are threaded on to copper wire, then wrapped around with more wire to create bangles and a necklace. Silver stars are secured on to the necklace using strong thread.

▼ Scrap Shoal

Iron wire was twisted and bound together using pliers to make this fishy jewellery. The bamboo, buttons, and varnished musical score sheet were wired into the fish shapes in the same way; the coins were drilled before being attached.

▲ Wooden Art

This sinuous wooden brooch is exuberantly decorated with painted spots, stripes, and squiggles, then studded with glued flat-backed gems for added sparkle.

▲ Heraldic Hat Pins

Inspired by heraldic shields and battle standards, these hat pins combine copper, silver, brass, and gold, using the techniques of fusing, patination, and etching, to create contrasting textures.

◄ Etched Metal

These intricately shaped and patterned steel and copper earrings draw upon medieval heraldic devices for their designs. Patterns are carefully etched in the metal with nitric acid, then the metal is highly polished to finish.

Contributors

The Author
pp. 70-71 top

Deborah Alexander
pp. 52-55
Tel: 01403 241563
14 Barrington Road
Horsham
West Sussex RH13 5SN

Julie Arkell
pp. 38-41; p. 48 bottom right;
p. 49 top left
Tel: 0171-916 6447
Unit W8
Cockpit Workshops
Cockpit Yard
Northington Street
London WC1N 2NP

Louise Baldwin
pp. 26-29
Tel: 0171-639 2765
18 Reynolds Road
London SE15 3AH

Victoria Brown
pp. 30-33; p. 47 bottom right
Tel: 0171-708 5559
88 Lyndhurst Grove
London SE15 5AH

Jane Burns
p. 91 bottom right
Tel: 0171-607 8043
265B Liverpool Road
London N1 1LX

Sheila Churchill/
Jacqueline Roberts
p. 70 left
Tel: 0181-994 4297
The Wild Jewellery Company
2 Mulberry House
Cavendish Road
London W4 3UH

Judy Clayton
pp. 42-45; p. 92 top left
Tel: 01273 603437
Flat 3
16 Lower Rock Gardens
Brighton
East Sussex BN2 1PG

Sally Cochrane
pp. 82-85; p. 91 top right
Tel: 01273 725321
14 Cross Street
Hove, East Sussex

Philippa Crawford
pp. 74-77; pp. 90-91 top
Tel: 0131-557 0109
26 Drummond Place
Edinburgh EH3 6PN

Sarah Crawford
p. 90 bottom left
Tel: 0181-340 6829
104B Hillfield Avenue
Crouch End
London N8 7DN

Alison Dane
p. 47 top right; p. 48 bottom right
Tel: 01359 258852
Crownlands Cottage
Walsham-le-Willows
Suffolk IP31 3BU

Lill Gardner
p. 69 top right
Tel: 0171-372 2502
22 Buckley Road
Brondesbury
London NW6 7NA

Janice Gilmore
pp. 34-37; p. 49 right
Tel: 01232 654867
28 Cyprus Park, Belfast
Northern Ireland BT5 6EA

Ray Halsall
pp. 64-67; p. 68 bottom left;
p. 69 bottom right
Tel: 0171-272 5164
14B Cressida Road
Archway, London N19 3JW

Deidre Hawken
p. 46 top
Tel: 0181-858 7091
35 Glenluce Road
Blackheath, London SE3 7SD

Tracy Hazlett
p. 48 top left; p. 90 top left
and bottom right
Tel: 01506 871235
16 Gloag Place
West Calder
West Lothian EH55 8DW

Gwen Hedley
pp. 18-21
Tel: 01494 873850
Oronsay, Misbourne Avenue
Chalfont St Peter
Buckinghamshire SL9 0PF

Julie Howells
p. 48 centre
Tel: 01344 773866
35 Greenwood Road
Crowthorne
Berkshire RG45 6JS

Lesley Anne Hutchings
pp. 68-69 bottom
Tel: 01273 774393
62a Goldstone Road
Hove, East Sussex BN3 3RH

Judy Ironside
pp. 14-17
Tel: 01273 540642
35 Claremont Terrace
Preston Park, Brighton
East Sussex BN1 6SJ

Helyne Jennings
p. 49 bottom left
Tel: 01769 520633
Pennyford Cottage
Burrington, Umberleigh
Devon EX37 9LN

Thérèse Kane
p. 93 top right
Tel: 01788 536352
11 Fellows Way
Hillmorton, Rugby
Warwickshire CV21 4JP

Diana Laurie
pp. 68-69 top; p. 69 centre;
p. 92 bottom right
Tel: 0171-831 6212
Unit 5, Cockpit Workshops
Cockpit Yard
Northington Street
London WC1N 2NP

Rachel Lucas/Ella Jennings
p. 47 bottom left
Tel: 0171-624 6812
Flat 2, 43 Aberdare Gardens
South Hampstead
London NW6 3AL

Rachel Maidens
p. 70 bottom
Tel: 01909 564408
51 Devonshire Drive
North Anston, Nr Sheffield
South Yorkshire S31 7AN

Louise Nelson
p. 47 top left
Tel: 01292 671626
9 Hillside Crescent
Prestwick, Ayrshire KA9 2JN

Polly Plouviez
pp. 56-59
Tel: 0171-916 0155
Unit W5, Cockpit Workshops
Cockpit Yard
Northington Street
London WC1N 2NP

Anna Pritchard
pp. 86-89; p. 93 bottom left
Tel: 0171-242 0519
Unit 4, Cockpit Workshops
Cockpit Yard
Northington Street
London WC1N 2NP

Lizzie Reakes
pp. 22-25; p. 46 bottom left
Tel: 0181-840 7579
68 Oaklands Road
Hanwell, Ealing
London W7 2DU

John Shortall
p. 71 right
26 Cooper Close
London SE1 7QU

Claire Sowden
p. 48 top right
Tel: 01252 870334
6 Bramling Avenue
Yateley, Camberley
Surrey GU17 7NX

Alison Start
pp. 78-81; p. 92 bottom left
Tel: 01273 674809
12 Arnold Street
Brighton
East Sussex BN2 2XT

Sam Vettese
pp. 92-93 top; p. 93 bottom left
Tel: 01506 880917
Almond House
Mid Calder
Lothian EH53 0AX

Sara Withers
pp. 60-63
Tel: 01865 862197
Old Cottage
Appleton, Abingdon
Oxfordshire OX13 5JH

Index

B

bangles *see* bracelets
beads 7, 8, 60-63, 68-71
    bracelets 69, 92
    choosing 60
    felt 30-33, 47
    glass 60, 70
    hat pins 91, 92
    paper 14-17, 48
    papier mâché 38-41
    polymer clay 52-55, 71
    threading 62-63
bell caps 10, 18
bracelets
    beaded 69, 92
    patchwork 26-29
    wire 69, 92
brass 82, 86, 92
brooches
    copper leaf 74-77
    embroidered 48, 82-85, 91
    hooked 22-25
    metal 78-81, 90, 91, 92
    mirror glass 64-67, 68, 69, 70
    modelling clay 68
    paper 47
    papier mâché 48
    vegetable 46
    wood 47, 93

C

cardboard 8
clay 52-55, 68, 71
copper leaf brooch 74-77
cufflinks 47

D

découpage 47
diamanté necklace 69

E

earrings
    embroidered 34-37, 46, 47, 48
    etched metal 86-89, 93
    fabric 46
    felt 47
    hooked 46
    metal 86, 90, 93

mirror glass 68
papier mâché 49
polymer clay 68
wire 90
embroidery 7, 9, 10
    brooch 48, 82-85, 91
    earrings 34-37, 46, 47, 48
    hat pin 42-45, 92
    pendant 49
enamel paint 78
equipment 7
etching
    brooch 91
    earrings 86-89, 93
    hat pin 93

F

fabrics 9, 13-49
fastenings 10, 18
felt 7, 9, 30-33, 47
findings 10
fleece 9, 30, 47
four-stranded necklace 60-63

G

glass 8, 51, 69, 70
    beads 70
    brooches 64-67, 68
    stained 9, 51, 56-59
glittering regalia brooch 64-67

H

hat pins 10, 42-45, 46, 91, 92, 93
hessian 9, 22
hooking 9, 22-25, 46

I

inks 9

K

kaleidoscope necklet 38-41
knitting needles 11, 14

L

leaves 8, 74-77

M

magic earrings 34-37
materials 7, 8-9
metal 7, 9, 72-93
    cutting/shaping 11, 80-81
    etched 86-89, 91, 93
    powders 47, 48
    soldering 11, 58-59, 77
millefiori mosaic beads 52-55
miniatures 73, 82, 90
mirror glass 8, 64-70, 68
mitres 77
mixed media brooch 82-85
modelling clay 68
mosaic 7, 8, 52
    brooch 64-67
muslin, vanishing 6, 9, 34-37, 42

N

necklaces
    see also pendants
    diamanté 69
    felt 30-33, 47
    four-stranded 60-63
    paper beads 14-17, 48
    papier mâché 38-41
    pebble 18-21, 70
    plastic tubing 48
    wire chain 90

P

paints 9
paper beads 14-17, 48
paper and fabric 8, 9, 13-49
papier mâché 8
    brooch 48
    earrings 49
    necklace 38-41
patchwork bangle 26-29
pebble necklaces 18-21, 70
pendants
    clay pipe 71
    diamanté 69
    embroidered 49
    silver 90
    stained glass 56-59
picture frames 7, 74-77, 82, 90, 91

plastic 7, 46, 90, 91
    cast 69
    PVC 42
    tubing 48
polishing 11
polymer clay 52-55, 68, 71
punching tools 11, 92
PVA glue 14

R

raffia 8, 9, 18-21
rag rug technique 13, 22-25, 46
recycling 7, 13, 22, 78, 91
renaissance riches hat pin 42-45
resin 7
rings 69

S

shells 18, 70
skewers 11, 14
solder 11, 58-59, 77
spot welder 78-81
stained glass 9, 51
    pendant 56-59
star-spangled stunner brooch 22-25
steel 78 81, 92

T

threading materials 8-9
tin brooch 78-81
tools 7, 10-11, 73
tubing 9, 48

V

vanishing muslin 6, 9, 34-37, 42
varnish 14, 41

W

wire 7, 8, 9, 10, 93
    bangles 69, 92
    earrings 90
    necklace 90
wood 8, 9, 73, 82-85, 93
wrapping 18, 20

Suppliers

The Bead Shop
43 Neal Street
Covent Garden
London WC2H 9JP
Tel: 0171-240 0831
Beads, findings, wire, and tools

Janet Coles Beads Ltd
Perdiswell Cottage
Bilford Road
Worcester WR3 8QA
Tel: 01905 755888
Beads, fastenings, threads, and tools (mail order)

Handweavers Studio & Gallery Ltd
29 Haroldstone Road
London E17 7AN
Tel: 0181-521 2281
Pre-dyed woollen fleece

James Hetley & Co Ltd
Glasshouse Fields
London E1 9JA
Tel: 0171-780 2346
Glass (mail order)

Lead & Light Coloured Glass
35A Hartland Road
London NW1 4BD
Tel: 0171-485 0997
Glass for mosaics

Silken Strands
c/o Catherine Spalding
20 Y Rhos, Penrhosgarnedd
Bangor, North Wales LL57 2LT
Tel: 01248 362361
Vanishing muslin, machine embroidery threads

J Smith & Sons
42-56 Tottenham Road
London N1 4BZ
Tel: 0171-241 2430
Sheet copper, brass, and steel

Acknowledgments

The most enormous thanks are due to the designers and jewellers who have dreamed up, refined, and perfected the sumptuous and sassy objects in these pages. The mark of a true creative spirit is an extraordinary generosity; every one of the artists and craftspeople who contributed to this book was happy to share hard won secrets and techniques with the world, probably because genuine innovators are always generating new ideas and moving on. Those of us who are not such creative powerhouses are in the happy position of being able to applaud and learn. In addition, the dedicated team who put this book together could not possibly be bettered: Clive Streeter took all the photographs with his usual perceptiveness and intelligence, and was an endless fount of good cheer and great ideas. He was efficiently helped out by Andy Whitfield, who also kept us fed and full of caffeine. Marnie Searchwell designed the book and was tirelessly perfectionist in her pursuit of faultless composition. Ali Edney sped around London in search of the essential props to show off the jewellery. That the whole unwieldy operation came together so brilliantly is entirely thanks to Heather Dewhurst, who documented every step with minute accuracy, and made it all comprehensible. Besides resulting in a handsome book, working with such a bunch of people is good for the soul and the giggle muscles.

The following companies kindly loaned props for photography:

The Bead Shop
43 Neal Street
Covent Garden
London WC2H 9JP
Tel: 0171-240 0831
Fastenings and tools

Cowling & Wilcox Ltd
26-28 Broadwick Street
London W1V 1FG
Tel: 0171-734 5781
Artist's materials

Fired Earth Tiles plc
21 Battersea Square
London SW11 3RA
Tel: 0171-924 2272
Slate tile on p.53

Liberty
Regent Street
London W1R 6AH
Tel: 0171-734 1234
Black wool jacket on p.31; wooden box on p.61; red wool crêpe jacket on p.65

Spread Eagle Antiques
8 Nevada Street
London SE10 9LJ
Tel: 0181-305 1666
Silver chain mail purse on p.87